WITHDRAWN

Computer Graphics
for Graphic Designers

COMPUTER GRAPHICS
for Graphic Designers

JOHN·VINCE

Knowledge Industry Publications, Inc.
White Plains, NY

Video Bookshelf

Computer Graphics for Graphic Designers

Library of Congress Cataloging in Publication Data

Vince, John
  Computer graphics for graphic designers.

  Bibliography: p.
  Includes index.
  1. Computer graphics. I. Title.
  T385.V558   1985
  006,6   85–19712

  ISBN 0–86729–162–1

Printed and bound in Great Britain

Contents

To Annie, Samantha and Anthony

Preface

It would not be an overstatement if I said that computer graphics was enjoying an unprecedented wave of popularity among practitioners of design-based disciplines. In some quarters one detects a sense of panic to the effect that if computer graphics is not used now, all is lost.

In education, schools, colleges, polytechnics and universities are attempting to raise substantial sums of money to ensure a place upon the computer graphic band-wagon. This enthusiastic activity reflects the confidence people have in the subject and the importance with which it is viewed. But those who have already attempted to join this 'high-tech' club have probably discovered how difficult it is to purchase, understand and use a technology that virtually becomes dated the day of installation.

This rapid growth is not only creating commercial problems but has also established pedagogic difficulties at all levels of academic development. For computer graphics provides us with such a sophisticated design facility that its immediate potential is overwhelming. At one end of the spectrum, the experienced user is seduced by state-of-the-art images from ray-tracing super computers, whilst at the other end—much nearer reality—the first-time user is struggling with the keyboard of a humble micro.

The subject is supported by some excellent books for the technical practitioner. But it has not been widely addressed by authors willing to take the time to explain what are basically simple concepts in everyday language. To redress the balance, I decided to produce this book, which attempts to introduce the design-based person—student and professional alike—to the concepts employed in computer graphic systems.

I have tried to maintain an air of simplicity throughout the book, without sacrificing accuracy. This has prevented me from employing the crisp precision of mathematical notation, but I hope that the descriptive substitute will still reveal the underlying simple ideas. Who knows, computer graphics might yet kindle a latent interest in mathematics and pro-gramming, and dramatically alter the reader's career.

In the author's own teaching experience, the teaching of computer graphics has awakened repressed skills in numeracy and problem-solving in many students, who have rapidly mastered this exciting subject, together with first-class design skills. This aspect of teaching is highly rewarding.

Above all, the reader should never accept that computer graphics is so technically complicated as to be impossible to comprehend. This is far from the truth. For if any barriers do exist, they have been caused by problems of communication, which will rapidly disappear as our understanding increases.

I wish to express my thanks to my students, who have directly and indirectly assisted in the development of this book, and to the companies which have supplied some of the illustrations: Cal Video Graphics Ltd, CalComp Ltd, Insight Terminals Ltd, Quantel Ltd, and the BBC; and to Don Knight, Paul Hughes, Keith Waters, and Liz Friedman for further pictures.

Finally, I must thank my wife for typing the original manu-script, Susanne Thackary and Heather Bliss for their editorial suggestions.

John Vince

Nazeing, 1985

1 Introduction

'The distance is nothing; it is only the first step that is difficult.'

Mme du Deffand

Today the very word 'computer' appears to surface in every aspect of our daily lives. We receive bills from computing systems; we complete forms which are processed by computers; we withdraw money from automatic cash dispensers with the permission of computers; we drive cars designed with the aid of computers and we enjoy video games simply because computer technology makes it all possible. But if they were to attempt to define or describe a computer, the majority of people would appear to believe in some super-human form of machinery with para-magical properties.

This mysticism is understandable, as the whole subject of computer technology has always been shrouded in mystery; ridiculous myths (generally created by the media and jargon which many would claim was deliberately chosen to ensure computer technology remained the esoteric science of engineers and mathematicians) have isolated the computer from the lay person. But, gradually, there is progress day-by-day towards a society which understands the principles of digital computing machinery, propelled by the education of young children who are being raised within a microcomputer-aided civilisation. For whether one likes it or not, computers seem to be here to stay and appear poised to shape the next phase of human development.

Computers have already been used to guide rockets, satellites and space shuttles with unbelievable accuracy. They have appeared in virtually every area of commercial and industrial enterprise and are now appearing in places where we least expected them. Television design departments and studios have wall-to-wall racks of digital equipment; architects, industrial designers, typographers, audio-visual artists, animators, interior designers, weavers and fine artists are beginning to employ computers, and now that this revolution has gained momentum there is a need to inform others of the benefits of using computers.

But before becoming totally overwhelmed by the computer's potential, one must remember to temper one's opinions with the disadvantages associated with computers. They are far from the ideal machine we imagine them to be—but more of this later.

So why does it appear that computers have suddenly jumped into our daily lives? Well, perhaps this might appear so to the layperson, but engineers and mathematicians should not be surprised. Arithmetic calculation has always been an essential component of their daily work for the past two or three thousand years and to them, the computer is nothing more than the result of a research and development programme which has been in progress for the past four thousand years.

A quick historical survey reveals that:

- The Babylonians (*circa* 2000 BC) solved sophisticated problems using mathematics. They were responsible for there being 360° in a circle, twenty-four hours to a day, and sixty seconds to a minute.

- Hindu (Indian) mathematics appears to have arisen from Babylonian and Hellenistic sources with some Chinese influence, and the Arabs who are credited with the concept of zero, perfected the decimal system used by the Hindus.

- Europe adopted the decimal numbering system during the ninth and tenth centuries. François Viète in the latter half of the sixteenth century used letters of the alphabet to denote abstract quantities and introduced the plus and minus signs. The multiplication sign appeared between 1600 and 1630 and the division sign about 1660.

- John Napier invented the idea of logarithms in 1614 but unfortunately died only three years later. However, Henry Briggs continued his work and published a table of logarithms in 1624. It is truly amazing that log tables were still in use in schools 350 years after their first printing. In 1620, Edmund Gunter conceived the idea of using sliding log scales to multiply and divide; later, in 1654, Robert Bissaker constructed the first practical slide rule.

- Although the abacus—probably of Babylonian origin—seems to have been the first digital register for counting, it was left to Blaise Pascal to invent the digital adding machine in 1642. Gottfried Wilhlem Leibniz invented a machine in 1671 which could multiply by repetitive addition. Further machines were developed by Léon Bollée and Charles Babbage who proposed the idea of machines driven by a program of instructions, i.e. a computer.

- During the 1940s, electrical relay machines were constructed by Bell Laboratories and other institututes, but were slow and unreliable. In 1945 the Moore School of Electrical Engineering built the all-electronic ENIAC computer which employed decimal notation. In 1950, John von Neumann used binary notation which established the foundations for all modern computer development.

- Also during 1950, simple pictures were displayed by the Massachusetts Institute of Technology's Whirlwind I computer, and in 1962 Ivan E. Sutherland submitted his doctoral dissertation, 'Sketchpad: A Man-Machine Graphical Computer System': computer graphics was born.

So we see that the computer has been a long time coming, but now that it has arrived we should attempt to understand its operation and how best it can be used. But it is not as straightforward as it might seem, for the explosive growth of microcomputers has created a world in itself. It has its own jargon of bits, bytes and ASCII code, plus new concepts of machine operation and speeds that baffle the lay mind. However, the task is not impossible, as we shall see. In fact, I hope that I shall be able to explain in everyday language how computers work and what role they play in assisting artists and designers.

Now, one of the keys to understanding any new subject is to master the jargon; and the learner should always bear in mind that it is an essential aspect of the subject, because frequently new words and phrases are necessary for labelling new concepts and processes. Just imagine the subject of graphic design, and consider how a non-designer relates to such terms as: air-brushing, cut and paste, three-colour separation, three-point perspective, drop shadows or silk screening. These words must appear as baffling to the non-designer as computer jargon might appear to a designer without computer training.

So, on with the book. But before we can begin thinking about how computers can be used to generate those fabulous coloured three-dimensional animated graphics, we must become familiar with the operating principles of computers, which is what the first chapter is concerned with.

2 Computer principles

'Where shall I begin, please your Majesty?' he asked.
'Begin at the beginning', the King said, gravely, 'and go on
till you come to the end: then stop.

Lewis Carroll

In this chapter I shall attempt to explain the operation of a
modern digital computer, but my first problem is to decide
upon the level of detail to include in my description. If I restrict
my explanation to a superficial overview, you will still be none
the wiser as to how a computer functions, and if I swamp you
with voluminous detail, you will not see the wood for the trees.
So I shall endeavour to transmit to you a simple, yet accurate,
description of a modern computer, employing the concepts
and jargon in current everyday use. All that I ask of you, the
reader, is to persevere and try to comprehend my description,
as I believe that an understanding of a computer's operation
will greatly influence your comprehension of computer
graphics.

2.1 Hardware and software

In the introduction to this book, I briefly outlined the historical
development of the computer, and traced its origins in the
early calculating machines which were an attempt to simplify
the tedious mathematical calculations encountered by
mathematicians, engineers, actuaries and scientists, etc.
Basically, the modern computer should be viewed as a simple
calculating machine, controlled by a memory unit storing a
sequence of instructions which it obeys. The stored instructions are called the program, and are held electronically within
the computer's memory. The larger the memory, the more
instructions can be held, which implies that the machine can
be used to undertake larger sequences of computation. So
already one can see that a computer system consists of two
basic elements: the hardware is the electronic machinery that

undertakes the calculation and manipulation of numbers, whilst the software is the sequence of instructions driving the machine; and no matter what computer you buy, if you are unable to supply the software, the machine is unable to function.

A common fallacy concerning computers, which many people believe, is that computers can solve problems by themselves. Well, that is ridiculous! One would no more ask questions of a television or dishwashing machine than ask a computer to predict the weather or the outcome of a horse race. But that is not to say that a computer is as limited as a dishwasher, because the latter has been designed and programmed only to wash dishes, whilst a computer is a general purpose programmable machine, and with the correct program can be used as an aid to solving a myriad of problems. For example, a computer used in conjunction with a payroll program can compute the weekly payslips of a company's employees, and also, with the aid of another program, predict the monthly sales of the company over the next twelve months. But this process is nothing magic—there happens to be a statistical technique for performing these predictions which can be computed with a pencil and paper. The computer simply removes the tedium from these calculations and provides an accurate answer rapidly.

Thus, a computer must be seen as a calculating tool used as an aid to solve a problem, the solution having been supplied by some intelligent external agency, namely us, human beings. There is no doubt that intelligent machinery will one day be available, but for the moment, any 'intelligent' problem-solving abilities are dependent upon very sophisticated programs.

One universal characteristic observable within our universe is that energy—whatever it is—is required to perform work. The sun radiates light by consuming vast quantities of its mass through atomic reactions, birds are able to fly by eating worms and other delicacies, and we are able to move and think by consuming air and food, which produce internal chemical reactions. A computer, on the other hand, must be supplied with a simple source of energy, namely electricity. Perhaps one day in the future, robots will have developed to the point

where they can be given a ham sandwich and a cup of coffee as a source of energy: then they could evolve just like us!
Electricity has many advantages, for example:

- It can be transmitted through metals and semi-conducting materials such as silicon.
- It can be stored chemically in batteries.
- It can cause magnetism and vice versa.
- It can create electrostatic fields and vice versa.
- It can be switched on and off rapidly.
- It travels very fast, approximately 100,000 miles per second.

But, unfortunately, it causes heat when it has to overcome any resistance to its movement. Even silicon chips, employed in computer circuitry, have to conduct relatively large amounts of electricity, and because of the internal resistances produce undesirable heat. In fact, some very large computers still require water cooling to remove this heat. However, in spite of this heating effect the advantages are considerable.

2.2 Information and codes

Electricity is used to transmit information throughout a computer's circuitry, and it is worth noting that the codes employed in modern computers were not those chosen by the original inventors. It was only through continuous experimentation that the binary coding system became the preferred system. But what is meant by a binary coding system? Perhaps the best way to understand it is to compare it with the Morse code invented by Samuel Morse in 1838, which is rapidly disappearing but which is still used for simple walkie-talkie systems.

Morse devised his code to permit the transmission of messages over a telegraphic system, and the code is shown in Figure 2.1. Morse, by the way, was also a respected painter in America, known for his sensitive portraits of prominent people. The letter 'A' is represented by the code · - (dot, dash) and sounds as one short bleep followed by a long one. An experienced operator can easily decode a continuous sequence of dots and dashes into text. Morse code is in fact a binary code, as it employs two states (a dot and a dash) to

A ·—	N —·	1 ·————	period	·
B —···	O ———	2 ··———	comma	——··——
C —·—·	P ·——·	3 ···——	colon	———···
D —··	Q ——·—	4 ····—	query	··——··
E ·	R ·—·	5 ·····	apostrophe	·————·
F ··—·	S ···	6 —····	hyphen	—····—
G ——·	T —	7 ——···	fraction bar	—··—·
H ····	U ··—	8 ———··	parentheses	—·——·—
I ··	V ···—	9 ————·	quotation	·—··—·
J ·———	W ·——	0 —————		
K —·—	X —··—			
L ·—··	Y —·——			
M ——	Z ——··			

Figure 2.1 The Morse Code

encode information. But computers, rather than using short dots and long dashes, employ sequences of electrical pulses of equal duration, and during one unit interval of time a pulse is either detected or not. For example, a common computer code assigned to the letter 'A' is 11100001, where 0 indicates the absence of a pulse and 1 represents a pulse. Electrically the signal would look like the waveform shown in Figure 2.2.

This method of encoding is much more convenient for electrical circuitry than the Morse code, because pulses are of equal length and they either exist or do not exist. Each pulse position is called a 'BIT' (BInary digiT). But how many bits are necessary to encode all the different letters of the alphabet? Let us approach the answer to this question in stages.

Imagine first, that only two bits are available; then there would be four possible code combinations: 00, 01, 10 and 11; and if three bits were available eight combinations would result: 000, 001, 010, 011, 100, 101, 110 and 111. The relationship between the code combinations and bits is very simple; perhaps you have already discovered it. In fact it is represented by the following formula:

$$2^{Bits} = \text{code combinations.}$$

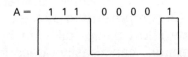

Figure 2.2 This waveform shows how the letter 'A' is stored electrically within a digital computer.

Which means that if 2 is multiplied by itself Bits number of times, the answer produces the code combinations. So to encode the twenty-six letters of the alphabet one requires at least five bits, providing thirty-two different code patterns. But a computer must also be able to handle numbers, which implies the need for an extra ten patterns 0 to 9. Therefore, six bits would be required giving sixty-four codes ($2 \times 2 \times 2 \times 2 \times 2 \times 2 = 64$), which is more than adequate. The spare patterns are in fact used for other symbols such as: " £ $ % & ' ( ) @ + * etc. This cluster of bits is called a byte.

Some early computers were constructed with a six-bit byte, but the majority of modern machines are now constructed with eight bits per byte, giving 256 code combinations. The number 256 will reappear later when we examine how computers encode colours in graphic systems, because bytes are also used to encode colour information.

So now we see that a fundamental structure of the computer code is the byte, which can encode all the possible symbols (upper-case and lower-case). The most popular coding system employed within the computing industry is ASCII: the American Standard Code for Information Interchange (pronounced 'as-ski').

Modern computer memories are fabricated upon silicon chips which are capable of storing tens of thousands of bytes of data. Figure 2.3 shows a silicon chip assembly employed in modern computing systems. But a computer's memory, apart from storing numbers and text, must be capable of holding the instructions which ultimately drive the machine. To encode these instructions, and their references to the computer's memory, more bits are necessary. The trend in modern computers is towards joining four bytes together giving thirty-two bits. This cluster of bits is called a word and holds one machine instruction.

So, on a 32-bit computer each instruction requires four bytes to hold it, whilst a 16-bit machine requires two bytes, but the 32-bit machine can work with larger memories and would typically operate faster.

The memory size of a computer is always specified in terms of its byte capacity, and as they might contain thousands or millions of bytes a special notation has evolved employing the letters 'K' and 'M'. '1 KByte' implies 1,024 bytes, whilst '1 MByte' (1 Mega Byte) represents 1,048,576 Bytes (1,024 × 1,024). The reason for this stems from the way memories are fabricated, which is in the form of a matrix of electrical elements. Notice that 32 × 32 = 1,024.

Modern microcomputers are constructed with memory sizes ranging from 16 KBytes to 128 KBytes, whilst minicomputers and main-frame computers vary between 1 MByte and 32 MBytes.

Figure 2.3 A modern encapsulated silicon chip showing pin connections.

2.3 Computer instructions

Up to now I have not mentioned the type of instructions found in a computer's memory, but they are very simple. One group of instructions (the arithmetic), undertakes additions, subtractions, multiplications and divisions, which can be performed on some machines at the rate of a million per second. Another group (the input and output commands), permits the computer to accept data from keyboards and other input devices, and also transmits from memory data for display upon terminals, etc. There are also other instructions that permit the computer to interrogate the contents of specific bytes of memory and take different actions depending upon their contents. One very special instruction is the GOTO command which forces the computer to leap-frog over other instructions and continue processing at another word in memory. For instance, a payroll program only requires sufficient instructions to compute one person's payslip, for when the program has been executed and the pay computed, a GOTO instruction forces the machine to return to the top of the program and repeat the same instructions, but with different data. This idea of repeating the program over and over again is vital in computer animation programs.

So before a computer can begin to function, a program of instructions must be organised within its memory in the correct sequence together with any data (numbers, names, addresses etc.). Great care must be taken to ensure that instructions and data do not become mixed together, because if the computer's processing unit was forced to extract a word of memory, which accidentally contained data, unpredictable behaviour would result!

Having discovered bits, bytes and words, perhaps it is time we examined the structure of a simple program. As an example, let us consider a program which can add any two numbers together and display the result. To begin with, the program must have two instructions which accept the numbers from a computer terminal, followed by instructions which perform the addition, and then a command which displays the answer. The program could be organised as follows:

Word

1: Input the first number into word 8.
2: Input the next number into word 9.
3: Load the contents of word 8 into an arithmetic register.
4: Add the contents of word 9 to the arithmetic register.
5: Store the contents of the arithmetic register in word 10.
6: Output the contents of word 10.
7: Stop.

Here is a detailed description of what happens.

Instruction 1
Wait for the user to input a number; when it is entered, place it in word 8 within the memory.

Instruction 2
Wait for the user to input another number; when it is entered, place it in word 9 within the memory.

Instruction 3
Place the contents of word 8 into another piece of memory called an arithmetic register.

Instruction 4
Add the contents of word 9 to the contents of the arithmetic register, leaving the result in the register.

Instruction 5
Store the contents of the arithmetic register into word 10 of the memory.

Instruction 6
Display upon the computer's terminal the contents of word 10.

Instruction 7
Stop the computer.

So we see that seven instructions are needed to perform the trivial task of adding two numbers together; just imagine the program sizes required to create coloured, shaded, three-dimensional scenes. These could run into tens or hundreds of thousands of instructions, and each one must be placed in its correct position. This must seem an impossible task, but there are certain programming techniques which make it relatively easy.

Before moving to another topic, it will be useful to follow the action of the above program with some sample data. For example, say that the first number entered was '3', this would be placed in word 8. If the second number entered was '6', this would be stored in word 9. The third instruction forces the computer to make a copy of word 8 (i.e. '3') into the arithmetic register. The 'add' instruction adds together '6' and '3' leaving the result '9' in the register. The fifth instruction transfers the number '9' to word 10, and finally, the answer '9' is displayed upon the terminal.

These instructions are obeyed at an unbelievable speed, typically one million every second. Therefore, if we are to obtain the maximum performance from a computer it should not have to depend too much upon human intervention, as we cannot operate at these speeds.

2.4 Computer languages

The ultimate language for any digital computing system is based upon the binary code, which, I can assure you, is not very convenient for human beings. And apart from that, computer manufacturers choose different codes to control their machines, which makes it virtually impossible to remember all the various coding systems for every available computer, not to mention the problems of software compatibility.

Figure 2.4 illustrates two imaginary versions of the above program, one expressed in a binary form and the other in ASCII format, where each byte is translated into a symbol. I can still remember using a computer where it was possible to enter a program on a punched card storing eighty bytes, and controlling it by entering a string of ASCII symbols. I must

1010010111001000	%	H
1010010111001001	%	I
1100000011001000	@	H
1011101011001001	:	I
1010111111001010	/	J
1010101111001010	+	J
1110000111000000	a	@
Binary	ASCII	

Figure 2.4 Machine code is stored internally using binary code, but can also be represented as bytes in the ASCII code. The above codes represent the way a program could be stored in some imaginary computer.

admit, however, that it took some time to design the program, but I was always amazed by the complexity of instructions which could be encoded within a few dozen symbols.

Obviously, this is not the optimum method of programming. Perhaps it is efficient from the computer's point of view, but is far too tedious from the human standpoint. Fortunately, during the evolution of computers, someone had the insight to employ the technique of language substitution, which greatly simplifies the programming function. For example, why should the above program not be expressed as follows?

```
Input    8
Input    9
Load     8   where 8, 9 and 10 refer
Add      9   to memory words
Store   10
Output  10
Stop
```

The logic expressed in the above code is identical to the preceding program, it is just expressed in another form. Therefore, there must be a simple procedure to translate one language into another. In fact, there is.

Programs were quickly developed to perform this translation and are called assemblers. They make programming a much easier task, as programmers can employ commands which are closer to natural languages used by human beings. Indeed, no sooner had the first assemblers been developed than further research into language translation created programs which could perform highly sophisticated translations; these are known as compilers. As an example, the language BASIC (Beginners All Symbolic Instruction Code) can be used to program a microcomputer as follows:

```
010 INPUT  X
020 INPUT  Y
030 LET    Z = X+Y
040 PRINT  Z
050 STOP
```

When these symbols are entered into a microcomputer and the command 'RUN' given, a special translator program examines every line and interprets the contents, and instructs the computer to obey the implied logic expressed within the symbols.

Perhaps you have already realised that there is no limit to the number of possible computer languages. In fact, anyone can invent a computer language, but someone must also create the necessary translator program to perform the translation into machine language, and there lies the problem. If a language is to be useful it must have a translator; it must be easy to use; have a long life; be available upon many computers; have adequate documentation and be supported by the computing industry; and this involves time and money. Consequently, the majority of software is implemented within a dozen or so high-level languages, some of the more popular being: APL, FORTRAN, BASIC, ALGOL, PASCAL, PL1, COBOL, ADA, C, SNOBOL, LISP, LOGO and CORAL.

Each language has been designed to meet the needs of specific problem areas, for example, FORTRAN (FORmula TRANslation) is for mathematicians and scientists, hence the name; whilst COBOL (COmmon Business Oriented Language) was developed to support business applications; so far no one has designed a universal high-level language to support computer graphics. Most computer graphic systems are still implemented in scientific languages such as FORTRAN, BASIC and PASCAL, etc. Perhaps with the advent of more sophisticated systems employing artificial intelligence, it will be possible for computers to respond to commands expressed in natural languages such as English and French—only time will tell.

2.5 Programming

Let us now examine how a modern computer is programmed. To begin with, a problem must exist requiring a solution; in a business situation this might be in the form of a system to keep check on company accounts and financial transactions; in a scientific application an engineer might wish to examine the stresses and strains a roof structure can withstand under different loadings, whilst a designer might wish to create ten seconds of 3D animation. Either problem must be first resolved by a programmer and expressed in the form of a program of instructions in some computer language. When this has been prepared, perhaps over a period of hours, days or weeks—depending on the problem's complexity—it is entered into a computer normally via a terminal and is translated into binary machine code. This translation might take approximately one minute.

If the translator program detects any errors in the use of the language, perhaps spelling mistakes or illegal characters, it reports on their position and stops. When the programmer has corrected the relevant errors, the program is again offered to the translator which might succeed in creating a binary version. If so, the computer is instructed to obey the binary commands and output the results. Who knows what will happen, perhaps the program functions correctly first time, but perhaps it contains obscure logical errors which must be corrected by the programmer before the program can be useful. However, when the program does begin to function and supply correct results it becomes an extremely powerful modelling tool. Just think of the financial controller who can investigate with great speed where the company's capital is stored, who owes money, and even anticipate cash-flow problems before they become too serious. What of the scientist who can alter a few parameters in the program which alter the positions and values of loads, and within a few seconds be supplied with new levels of stress and strain?

But how can a designer benefit from the computer? Well, as we shall see later on, the computer could supply an animated sequence of 3D scenes, but if the movement was too fast or slow, just by altering one or two numbers, the computer could rerun the program with different data and create totally new images. This indeed is a powerful design facility.

Although there are many problems in computer graphics which require original programs before any pictures are produced, there are, however, many instances where computers are pre-programmed to perform specific functions. For example, Quantel's Paint Box system is pre-programmed to enable users to create coloured two-dimensional scenes upon a television screen. It can also, with extra software, be used to animate elements of the picture and display the animation in real-time. But it would be impossible to make it display three-dimensional scenes using its standard software, as the programs are not designed to meet these requirements. Indeed, other systems are available which could display 3D images, but they would probably be unable to offer a painting facility. Similarly, an architectural computer design system would be programmed to meet the specific needs of an architect. Thus we see that computer-based graphic systems are no different from conventional computer systems, they are simply equipped with adequate programs to make them useful to the user.

2.6 Computer systems

Before we leave this chapter I should try to establish a unified image of a typical computer system, because so far, I have relied heavily upon words to communicate the action of the machine.

It has often been said within the industry that once you have seen one computer you have seen them all, but I do not think this is strictly true today. Computers are manufactured in all shapes and sizes; on single silicon chips, within childrens' toys, micros, mini commerical systems right up to the massive super computers. So, in Figure 2.5 you will see a popular general-purpose computer, widely used for computer graphic applications. Notice that it is just a couple of cabinets storing the essential circuitry which performs the programmed computations.

This central processing unit is connected to a stable power supply and often installed in a clean and humidity-controlled environment. Connected to the central processor are one or more cables, which transmit the signals to and from the user-terminals. These could be positioned locally, say within several dozen metres, or virtually anywhere else in the world with the aid of communications equipment. But if several people began typing commands simultaneously into the central processor, it would be unfair to expect any response, because how could the system keep a record of which signal came from which terminal? It would also have no way of coping with the various languages used by different users.

Figure 2.5 This modern minicomputer is often employed in computer graphic systems.

Remember, the computer is a machine without any super-human facilities.

Before the computer can be used effectively by several users and programmed in various languages, it must itself be programmed to provide these services. Fortunately, when one buys a computer, this important program, called the Operating System, is supplied with the machine and includes the language translators required by the users. During the normal daily operating schedule of the computer, part of the operating system program is resident in the memory and can consume a considerable amount of space, perhaps 10 to 20 per cent; the rest remains on magnetic disk units, which are capable of holding several hundred million bytes of data. These rotating disks can be automatically accessed by the central processor in a few thousandths of a second and can be updated by over-writing the original information. Figure 2.6 shows a photo-graph of a disk pack which is capable of storing approximately 200 Megabytes of data.

Now, when anyone wishes to use the computer they can only do so with the permission of the operating system, and it

Figure 2.6 A computer accesses its data stored upon magnetic disk packs. This pack stores approximately 200 Megabytes.

is worth remembering that every operating system differs from machine to machine. The operating system is an extremely complex program and is generally designed by a team of programmers. It typically provides the user with the following facilities:

- maintenance of files (programs and data);
- security and integrity of stored data;
- translation of high-level language programs into machine code;
- execution of programs;
- file creation;
- program development and testing facilities.

Before any work can be started, a user must be identified by the operating system; only then is the user given access to previously stored information held on the disks. The user continues to control the computer by issuing commands to the operating system that undertakes the work.

Very often a computer appears to make human-like comments in reply to a user's instructions, something along the lines: 'Please enter the file name again, thank you' or 'Disk quota exceeded, please contact the computer manager'. These must not be taken as an invention of the hardware, they have been included within the software from the very start, carefully placed by a programmer to ensure that the system appears friendly and understanding. I am sorry if this clinical explanation of the computer's behaviour has removed the fantasy that often surrounds these systems, but they must be seen as machines. Nevertheless, in spite of this, it is still difficult to prevent the computer entirely from having its own personality.

2.7 Summary

The important points covered so far are as follows:

- The computer is an electronic calculating machine driven by a stored program of instructions.

- Hardware describes the machinery, whilst software describes the programs.

- The instructions are encoded within a binary system consisting of bits.

- The same binary code is used to encode data (letters, symbols and numbers) in clusters of eight bits, i.e. bytes.

- One instruction typically requires four bytes (thirty-two bits).

- Instructions are obeyed at the rate of approximately one million per second.

- Instructions are available to perform additions, subtractions, multiplications, comparisons, input and output, GOTO and STOP, etc.

- High-level languages have been developed to express the solution to problems in a form convenient to humans.

- Translator programs are available to translate high-level language programs into binary machine code.

- The operating system program permits several users to undertake simultaneous work and perform complex programming tasks with the minimum of effort.

- Some computer graphic systems are pre-programmed and therefore can only undertake actions incorporated within their software.

3 2D computer graphics

'I have often admired the mystical way of Pythagoras and the secret magic of numbers.'

Sir Thomas Browne

In the previous chapter we discovered the characteristics of computer systems; now we must examine how they can assist in the field of design. At first sight there does not appear to be any connection between the two disparate disciplines; on the one hand, computers are mechanistic and mathematical, and, on the other hand, design is associated with creativity and artistic activities. None the less, I would not be surprised if computers turned out to be the most influential design tool ever used by artists and designers. Already, during their very short existence, computers have revolutionised the television industry, and computer aided design (CAD) systems are rapidly becoming a natural part of design studios. I wonder what their influence will be in a hundred years time?

One essential phase of computerising any activity, whether it is commercial, scientific, mathematical or artistic, is to understand the activity in terms of its components and their manipulation. Returning once more to the payroll example, a programmer must be aware of the procedures used to calculate pay (that is, tax calculations, national insurance, overtime, pension, allowances, etc.), before a program can be constructed to perform these calculations. Likewise, the computerisation of a design activity requires a basic understanding of the concepts employed by designers and how they are manipulated before any program can be formulated. So how does a designer go about solving a problem? That is a demanding question but let me attempt to answer it even if my efforts are incomplete.

I suppose that when a designer is faced with a problem there is a period of contemplation when ideas are examined, manipulated and perhaps rejected, but finally a solution may be produced which satisfies the initial specification. Some people might be able to perform this function without any external aid, whereas others might require to make sketches as an idea is manipulated and honed into shape. This sketching or doodling stage is where the computer could possibly assist; but what facilities would the designer require? Again, this is another demanding question but a few ideas are proposed in the following sections and others can be added later.

3.1 2D system requirements

To start with, there would be no point in using any system, computerised or not, if it could not provide the basic drawing features offered by a pencil, paper and eraser. So any computerised system must provide:

- the ability to input and display line drawings rapidly; and
- the possibility of correcting the image.

But it would also be useful if it could provide:

- assistance in the drafting operations for handling curves, ellipses, circles, etc.;
- the definition of linear measurements and angles;
- the cross-hatching of shapes.

All of these facilities can be provided by computer graphic systems, but we are only asking the machine to mimic the actions of a pencil, ruler, pair of compasses and French curves. There are many other facilities one would like, and one is tempted to refrain from asking as they might not be possible; but at this stage we should not be afraid to ask for the impossible. Let us continue and identify anything that a designer might require:

- the mixing and application of colour;
- the creation of patterns;
- the introduction of external images;
- the ability to work in two and three dimensions;
- a facility to control perspective;
- the ability to alter textures and surface details;
- the ability to animate images.

But we shall have to stop, as the list could continue indefinitely. Nevertheless, the initial question has identified some important concepts that somehow must be expressed in computer instructions, one way or another.

Here then is one of the major problems of using computers in a highly visual and artistic activity. On the one hand we have discovered that a computer works arithmetically and mechanistically, and on the other, the area of application is an expression of our sensitivity and appreciation of shape, form, colour, balance and beauty. How then can the machine be coerced into manipulating such delicate concepts? The answer to this question is 'with some difficulty', but it is possible.

If the computer is to provide the above requirements a mechanism must be found to represent them accurately within its memory. For example, even to make the machine draw a straight line, a program must exist to control this process. What indeed are the programming procedures for mixing colours, controlling perspective, generating three-dimensional pictures and displaying animated coloured scenes? The answers will be revealed all in good time, but first we must examine some fundamental ideas that form the basis of computer graphic systems.

3.2 The coding of drawings

Now that we have seen the magnitude of the problem, we must proceed carefully, starting with some simple ideas that will permit a complete understanding of the most sophisticated effects outlined above.

To start with, a mechanism must be found which permits line drawings to be stored within a computer's memory. Fortunately, this is relatively easy, as mathematicians have been employing the technique for about three hundred years. The idea was invented by the French philosopher and mathematician René Descartes (1596–1650) who developed a method of representing graphically the relationships expressed by equations. I will not attempt to explain this procedure here— even though it is quite simple—but will just describe the underlying technique that is employed in computer graphics.

The name given to Descartes's invention is Cartesian co-ordinates. Notice it bears his name. It works as follows. Imagine the problem of specifying the location of a point on a flat map, so that the definition was precise and unique. One might be inclined to suggest some form of grid referencing, where the map is covered with a pattern of regular horizontal and vertical lines, as shown in Figure 3.1. The spot marked by an asterisk (*) could be identified by the references B,3 where B implies that the point is somewhere within the vertical strip referenced by B, and also within the horizontal strip referenced by 3. This approach is not very precise, nevertheless, it embodies the ideas of Cartesian referencing.

A more accurate and generalised procedure is illustrated in Figure 3.2. Here we see the introduction of a pair of axes inter-secting at 90°. This point is called the origin. The horizontal

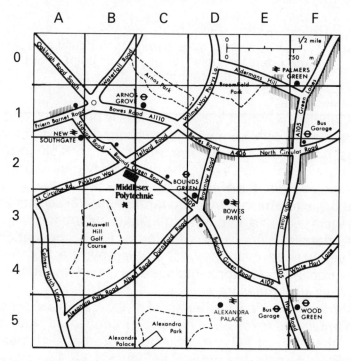

Figure 3.1 A useful way of locating a point on this map is to partition the area into horizontal and vertical strips, and identify the two strips containing it. The point marked by an asterisk has codes (B,3).

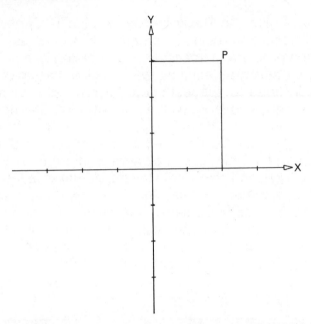

Figure 3.2 The intersecting axes identify the origin which becomes the reference point for any other point. The point P is identifed by the coordinates (2,3).

axis is labelled X, whilst the vertical axis is labelled Y, and both are graduated with some scale, perhaps in inches or centimetres, but the units are not important. It is possible to specify precisely any point relative to the origin by two measurements called the coordinates of the point. For example, the point P in Figure 3.2 is referenced by the coordinates, 2,3. i.e. it is 2 units along the X-axis and 3 units up the Y-axis; where the two references intersect identifies the location of P. A convention has been established over the years, whereby, the first number always implies the X-horizontal measurement and the second is the Y-vertical measurement.

Exploring this idea further quickly exposes two problems which must be resolved. The first is concerned with those points that do not fall precisely upon the units of measurement. For example, the point Q in Figure 3.3 is 1.5 units along the X-axis and 2.5 units along the Y-axis, therefore we must be prepared to use decimal numbers. So the decimal coordinates of Q are defined as (1.5, 2.5).

But the second problem is illustrated by Figure 3.4, where the point R also appears to have the same coordinates as P, i.e. (2.0, 3.0). So, to prevent this duplication it is necessary to introduce the idea of negative and positive coordinates. The established convention requires that measurements to the left and below the origin are negative, whilst to the right, and above, are positive. Consequently, the coordinates of R are (−2.0, 3.0). Similarly, the coordinates of S are (−2.0, −3.0).

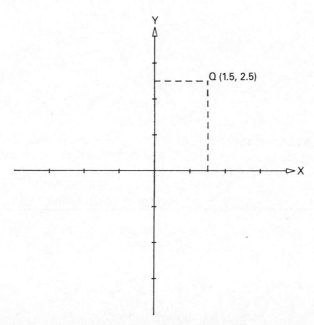

Figure 3.3 The point Q requires decimal numbers to locate it as it does not fall upon the units marked upon the axes. Its coordinates are: (1.5, 2.5).

So there we have a perfect mechanism for locating points upon a surface. Our initial problem was to encode line drawings, and Cartesian coordinates solve this problem very neatly. Consider the shape of the letter 'T' illustrated in Figure 3.5. If every corner of the shape is specified by its coordinates, they

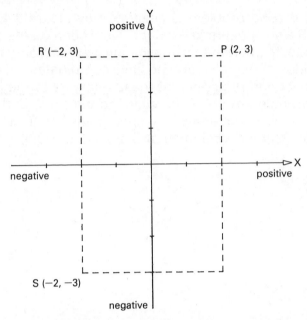

Figure 3.4 Coordinates to the left and below the origin are negative, whilst to the right and above are positive.

could be stored within a computer as two lists of numbers as follows:

X	Y
−1	−2
−1	1
−2	1
−2	2
2	2
2	1
1	1
1	−2

Notice that if you follow the path of the above coordinates, the original shape is traced out in a clockwise sense, starting from the bottom left-hand corner. The starting point and direction of the coordinates are not important at the moment, but it is important that the coordinates are in a sequence that make a complete uninterrupted journey around the shape.

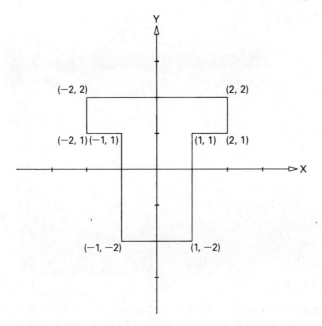

Figure 3.5 This shape of a letter 'T' can be represented by the coordinates of its corners.

Figure 3.6 shows a photograph of a machine called a graph plotter which, when connected to a computer, can be driven by a sequence of Cartesian coordinates moving a pen over a sheet of paper. Mechanically the plotter is extremely simple, but contains some clever electronic circuitry capable of computing straight lines between successive pairs of coordinates. So we can see that it is the graph plotter, and similar display devices, which reconstitute the original design by linking the coordinates with straight lines.

I wonder whether you have already noticed that if the above list of coordinates is plotted, the drawing will not correspond exactly to the original; in fact it will look like the shape shown in Figure 3.7. As the pen does not return to its starting point automatically, it must be driven there by repeating the first point as a final point. So in fact nine pairs of coordinates are required to produce the original closed shape.

This idea of Cartesian coordinates is fundamental to computer graphics, so before proceding it is worth examining one

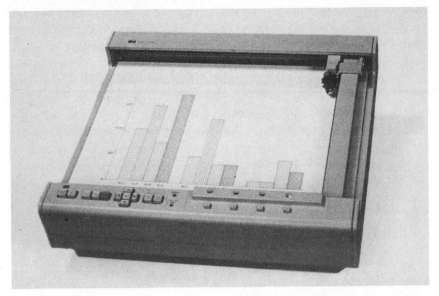

Figure 3.6 This graph plotter creates an image by joining a sequence of coordinates together with straight lines.

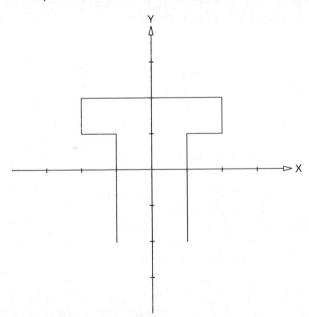

Figure 3.7 Even though the letter 'T' was defined by eight pairs of coordinates, the last line will not be drawn unless the plotter is instructed to return to the first point.

more example. Figure 3.8 shows the letter 'H' together with a list of coordinates. Notice that the first point has been repeated to close the shape.

Up to now, I have only considered extremely simple shapes, but there is nothing to prevent very complex designs from

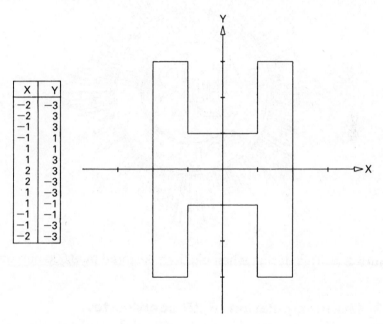

X	Y
−2	−3
−2	3
−1	3
−1	1
1	1
1	3
2	3
2	−3
1	−3
1	−1
−1	−1
−1	−3
−2	−3

Figure 3.8 This letter 'H' can be represented by thirteen coordinate pairs.

being stored in coordinate form. As an example, the design shown in Figure 3.9 requires 9,000 numbers to encode it; this might appear considerable, but for a computer it would only take a fraction of a second to process these numbers. Later on we shall examine the different methods of displaying lists of coordinates, but for the moment, it is sufficient to accept the existence of such devices so that we can concentrate on how the computer can manipulate coordinates.

Figure 3.9 This design when digitized is stored by 9,000 numbers.

3.3 The manipulation of 2D coordinates

There would be no point in storing coordinates within a computer unless it could perform something extra with them that could prove useful to us. So let us examine some of the simple arithmetic operations possible using a computer.

Without knowing how it is achieved, assume that it is possible to place within a computer's memory a list of coordinates; and to keep the description simple, we shall continue to manipulate the letter 'T' as shown previously in Figure 3.5.

The coordinates are as follows:

X	Y
−1	−2
−1	1

−2	1
−2	2
2	2
2	1
1	1
1	−2
−1	−2

But say they were manipulated by a program which added 1 to every X-coordinate, but left the Y-coordinates untouched. The resulting numbers would be:

X	Y
0	−2
0	1
−1	1
−1	2
3	2
3	1
2	1
2	−2
0	−2

The inquisitive person might be asking what the image would look like if it were drawn. Well, the resulting image is shown in Figure 3.10. Notice that the image has shifted one unit to the right. Furthermore, there is no need to resort to higher mathematics to prove that if we had added 2 to the X-coordinates, the shift would have been two units. Further reflection will confirm that subtracting a number will shift the image to the left.

Having shown the graphical effects resulting from modifying the X-coordinates, surely it is reasonable to assume that corresponding effects would result if the Y-coordinates were modified; that is, adding a number to the Y-coordinates shifts the image vertically, whilst subtracting lowers it.

So, we can confidently predict that a computer could be used to position an image anywhere upon some graphic display device simply by adding or subtracting numbers, to or from the list of coordinates. And as some machines function at the rate of several hundred thousand numbers per second,

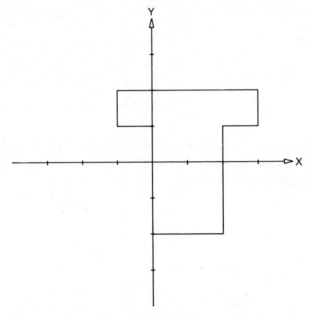

Figure 3.10 The effect of adding one to every X-coordinate is to shift the image one unit to the right.

with the aid of a fast display screen it is possible to display images that move continuously in real-time.

Having considered the add and subtract instructions, it seems natural to consider the effect of multiplication and division. Returning to the original list of coordinates encoding the letter 'T', consider the action of doubling every X-coordinate. The following list shows the result of this operation:

X	Y
−2	−2
−2	1
−4	1
−4	2
4	2
4	1
2	1
2	−2
−2	−2

If these are displayed, the shape shown in Figure 3.11 results. Notice that the width of the shape has doubled, and that the size change is relative to the origin, i.e. if one of the shape's points happened to be on the origin, it would remain there after modification, as zero times any number is still zero.

Without labouring this example, we should be able to reason that:

- multiplying the X-coordinates by three, trebles the width;
- dividing the X-coordinates by a number greater than 1 reduces the width;
- multiplying or dividing the Y-coordinates causes corresponding changes in the height.

This manipulation of coordinates is fundamental to computer graphic systems, therefore the reader should understand the above examples before proceeding.

Now in the preceding chapter we discovered that computers have a natural facility for performing additions, subtractions, multiplications and divisions at a tremendous speed, and

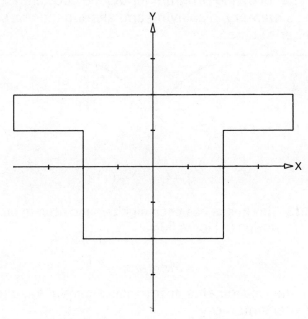

Figure 3.11 The original letter 'T' is stretched horizontally by a factor of 2 when its X-coordinates are doubled.

already we have seen the graphical implications of manipulating lists of coordinates using these instructions. They could be summarised by saying that adding and sub-tracting control position, but multiplying and dividing control size.

Even with these commands alone a computer can be used to create some interesting effects and provide useful drafting facilities, so before continuing let us consider what can be achieved with our current knowledge.

3.4 Simple image manipulation

In the following examples I am going to propose the outline of two programs which exploit the machine's ability to add, subtract, multiply and divide.

Example 1

Figure 3.12 shows an image which has been transformed into coordinate form and stored within a computer's disk filing system. The following program inputs the coordinates into the computer's memory, displaying and altering their size a speci-fied number of times.

Figure 3.12 This image has been digitized and used to produce the design in Figure 3.13.

Program

(a) Input the coordinates from disk and place them in the computer's memory.
(b) Repeat stages (d) to (e) twenty times.
(c) Stop the computer.

(d) Display the coordinates.
(e) Multiply the coordinates by 1.05.

The output of this program is shown in Figure 3.13.

Figure 3.13 Here we see the effect of repeatedly increasing the
image size by 1.05.

Example 2

This example demonstrates the effect of repeatedly displaying
an image in different positions; in fact each position is determined by actual coordinates forming the original shape.

Program

(a) Input the coordinates from disk and place them in the
     computer's memory.
(b) Make a copy of the numbers in memory and divide these
     by twelve to reduce their size.
(c) Display the smaller image at every coordinate position of
     the original design.

The result of this program is shown in Figure 3.14.

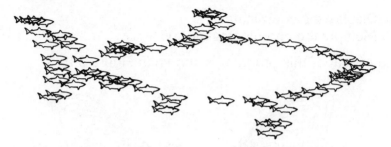

Figure 3.14 This design has been created by drawing a small version of a shark at every vertex of the shark.

The above examples, although very simple, indicate how the computer might be used in textile and pattern design, perhaps relieving the designer of the necessity of making tedious repetitions to achieve an effect.

3.5 Image reflections

Another useful mathematical operation is the reversal of a number's sign, i.e. if it is negative make it positive and vice versa. Consider the design shown in Figure 3.15 and the corresponding coordinates listed below:

X	Y
1	1
1	4
2	4
2	2
3	2
3	3
4	3
4	1
1	1

If the signs of the X-coordinates are reversed, what results graphically? The new coordinates would be:

X	Y
−1	1
−1	4

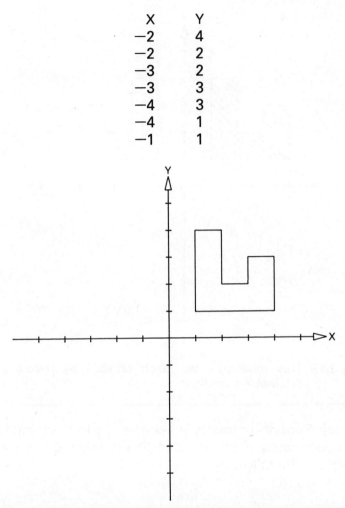

X	Y
−2	4
−2	2
−3	2
−3	3
−4	3
−4	1
−1	1

Figure 3.15 This irregular shape will be used to illustrate how reflections are created by sign reversals.

and the resulting image is shown in Figure 3.16. Observe that this sign reversal has produced a mirror image about the Y-axis. It is left as an exercise for the reader to confirm that reversing the signs of the Y-coordinates causes a similar mirror reflection about the X-axis.

If the signs of both X- and Y-coordinates are reversed, the image appears reflected in the quadrant diagonally opposite. Figure 3.17 illustrates all three reflections.

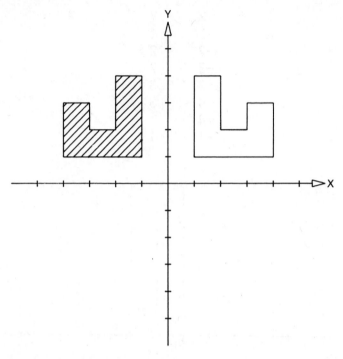

Figure 3.16 This reflection has been created by reversing the original X-coordinates.

Another form of symmetry is achieved by exchanging the X- and Y-coordinates. If this is done to the original coordinates used above, the following list is formed:

X	Y
1	1
4	1
4	2
2	2
2	3
3	3
3	4
1	4
1	1

The result of this exchange is shown in Figure 3.18. A reflection still results, but this time it is about an axis inclined at 45°.

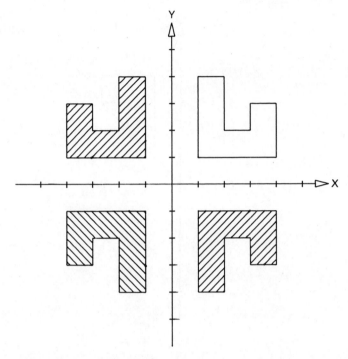

Figure 3.17 These three reflections are formed by reversing the X- and Y-coordinates.

Now the reversal of signs only produces reflections about the X- and Y-axes. If a reflection is required about an axis, orientated at any angle, the mathematics becomes slightly more complicated and actually requires sines and cosines to resolve the geometry. This, however, should not concern us, for as long as we realise that it is possible that is all that matters.

Another similar form of manipulation is concerned with image rotation, so let us examine these ideas.

3.6 Rotation of images

So far we have explored the effects of incrementing and multiplying, and that of sign reversal of coordinates, discovering that each process causes a predictable graphic effect. There are many more operations one can perform with numbers but

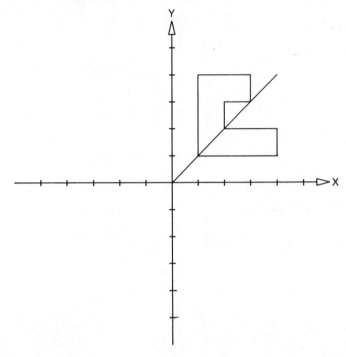

Figure 3.18 The operation of exchanging coordinates effectively reflects the image about a line at 45°.

unfortunately they require an understanding of some mathematical techniques. In the following explanation, only simple mathematics will be used.

Rotating an image by multiples of 90° is a relatively simple operation. For example, to rotate by 90° the coordinates are manipulated in two stages; first the coordinates are exchanged and the signs of the X-coordinates are reversed. A mathematician would express this operation as follows:

$$X_{90} = -Y$$

$$Y_{90} = X$$

The original set of coordinates used above would become:

X	Y
−1	1
−4	1

X	Y
−4	2
−2	2
−2	3
−3	3
−3	4
−1	4
−1	1

This image is shown in Figure 3.19.

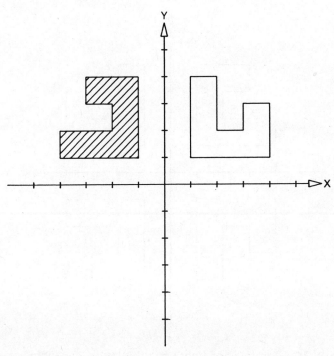

Figure 3.19 Any image can be rotated anti-clockwise 90° by applying the following operations: $X_{90} = -Y$, $Y_{90} = X$

Again, without labouring the point it can be shown that a rotation of 180° is produced by:

$$X_{180} = -X$$

$$Y_{180} = -Y$$

and by 270°:

$$X_{270} = Y$$

$$Y_{270} = -X$$

Figure 3.20 shows all three rotations. Notice that these rotations are not the same as the reflections.

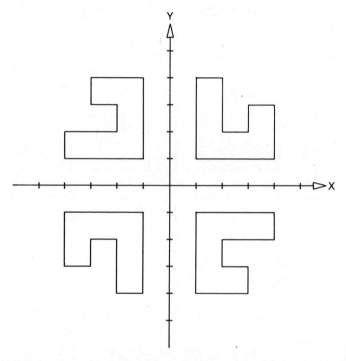

Figure 3.20 Simple coordinate manipulation can achieve rotation of 90°, 180° and 270° about the origin.

But how can the image be rotated say by 60°, or any other angle? The formula is given here but the proof that it produces the correct results is omitted (the more mathematical reader can provide his or her own proof). So, given any point P with coordinates X, Y the new point P′ with coordinates X′, Y′ is computed by the formula:

$$X' = X \cdot \cos Q - Y \cdot \sin Q$$

$$Y' = Y \cdot \cos Q + X \cdot \sin Q$$

where Q is any angle.

This might look frightening if one has forgotten the ideas of trigonometry, but it would not present any problems to a graphic programmer. The above equations are illustrated graphically in Figure 3.21.

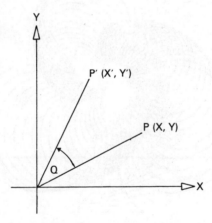

Figure 3.21 Any point P with coordinates (X, Y) can be rotated about the origin by an angle Q to produce a new point P′ (X′, Y′).

3.7 Further image manipulation

Now that reflections and rotations have been covered, perhaps it would be worth considering two further programs.

Example 3

This program produces the image shown in Figure 3.23 and is formed by repeatedly drawing, rotating and scaling the design in Figure 2.22. The program is as follows:

Figure 3.22 This design is used to create the image in Figure 3.23.

Figure 3.23 This design has been created by repeatedly: drawing, rotating, and scaling the image shown in Figure 3.22.

Program

(a) Input the coordinates from disk and place them in the computer's memory.
(b) Repeat stages (d) to (f) twenty times.
(c) Stop.
(d) Display the coordinates.
(e) Rotate the coordinates by 5°.
(f) Multiply the coordinates by 1.05.

Example 4

This program exploits the process of reflections and drawing a regular pattern.

Program

(a) Input the coordinates from disk and place them in the computer's memory.
(b) Create three reflections from the original design and store the coordinates.
(c) Repeat the total image at regular positions.
(d) Stop.

The original design is shown in Figure 3.24 and the final scaled image shown in Figure 3.25.

At this stage I think that it would be reasonable to take stock of the important ideas that have surfaced in this chapter. The most important idea I am trying to communicate is that the computer is a machine, and that everything, and I must stress everything, we demand from computerised systems must be programmed.

As the machine is conceptually blind, forcing it to undertake graphical problems means that visual and physical procedures must be carefully modelled numerically within the computer. I hope that I have successfully demonstrated that position, size, angle and reflections can all be implemented with relatively simple actions upon lists of coordinates; but there are many other important graphic procedures whose implementation are beyond the scope of this book.

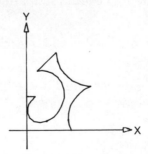

Figure 3.24 This motif has been digitized to create the effect in Figure 3.25.

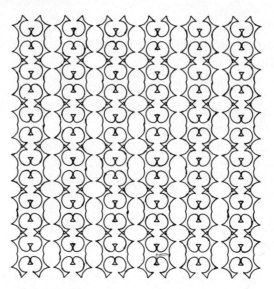

Figure 3.25 This pattern has been generated from the shape shown in Figure 3.24 using reflections and regular repetitions.

3.8 Summary

The following ideas have been discussed in this chapter:

- Line drawings are encoded numerically using Cartesian coordinates.

- Adding or subtracting numbers to and from coordinates effectively shifts the image.

- Multiplying or dividing coordinates effectively alters the size of the image.

- Simple reflections are achieved by exchanging or reversing signs of coordinates.

- Image rotations are obtained by exploiting the trigonometric functions sines and cosines.

4 Computer graphic peripherals

'Drawing is the true test of art.'
J. A. D. Ingres

In this chapter it is time to examine some of the special graphic peripherals associated with modern computer graphic systems, for they play an extremely important role in interfacing a user to a computer program.

Basically, peripherals divide into two groups: they are either concerned with transmitting actions to a program, or displaying output to the user.

The only machine so far mentioned has been the graph plotter, but I would like to begin with an input device which generates the vital coordinates.

4.1 The digitizer

A digitizer is an active surface which electronically computes Cartesian coordinates. Figure 4.1 illustrates a large digitizer capable of resolving measurements to +/−0.002". Beneath the white plastic surface is encapsulated a matrix of horizontal and vertical wires radiating a low-level radio signal. When an operator places a puck or pen, shown in Figure 4.2, on any desired position and presses a button, a signal is detected by a small coil of wire hidden within the puck or pen, which is given to a microcomputer to translate into Cartesian coordinates. The illustrated digitizer—like many others—has various modes of operation; the one just described is called the 'point' mode, where one point is computed each time a button is pressed. In a, 'track' mode, whenever the stylus or puck is activated, the microcomputer automatically samples the position of the pen; this might be at the rate of one to one hundred times per second. This enables drawings to be digitized simply by tracing around the contours.

A digitizer cannot just be connected to a computer without some software mechanism to control its output. If, for

Figure 4.1 A large digitizer used for creating Cartesian coordinates from artwork. (Courtesy of Terminal Display Systems Ltd)

example, it is used to digitize some design, a program is required to accept the generated coordinates and store them on a disk file. The program might provide facilities to display that part of the design digitized so far; or to input regular shapes such as circles, rectangles, ellipses, arcs, etc., and perhaps the ability to correct mistakes introduced by faulty digitizing.

Small digitizers, normally called tablets, are very useful in computer graphic workstations. The one shown in Figure 4.3 is used to command a computer aided design system. An operator controls the computer by pointing at a menu of commands; when a command is given, the program receives a pair of coordinates which are compared with other coordinates stored internally. Depending upon the zone digitized, the program decides the action to be undertaken by the computer.

The action of digitizing is generally very tedious. Just

Figure 4.2 A stylus or puck must be used in conjunction with a digitizer to identify a point. (Courtesy of CalComp Ltd.)

imagine the time and concentration required to trace every continent, island and lake making up the map of the world illustrated in Figure 4.4.

When the design to be digitized is regular and consists of long straight lines, the artwork need not be too precise as only the lines' endpoints are required; but when the design is irregular and consists of delicate curves, it is essential to take precautions to minimize the introduction of errors. Basically, there are three sources of error: first, the artwork may not be precise; secondly, the person digitizing will introduce a random personal error; and lastly, the digitizer introduces its own inherent error. To keep the total error to a minimum, the artwork is generally drawn two or three times too large, and as the human and the digitizer error is independent of this size, the coordinates and any error can be reduced by scaling them down in a program.

Figure 4.3 This CAD system is controlled via menus placed over a digitizing tablet. (Courtesy of CalComp Ltd.)

Figure 4.4 This map of the world was digitized from an A0 map and is stored as 7,000 coordinate pairs.

4.2 The graph plotter

As mentioned briefly in the previous chapter, a graph plotter reconstitutes an image by tracing out straight lines between successive pairs of coordinates. To prevent all coordinates from being linked together continuously, extra commands must accompany them to control when the pen should lift and touch the paper. Figure 4.5 illustrates a belt graph plotter which is capable of drawing long lines at speeds in excess of 1 metre per second and to an accuracy of 0.005″. The smallest increment made by the pen is also 0.005″ which means that very smooth detailed artwork can be plotted accurately and very fast.

Graph plotters are manufactured in all shapes and sizes. Drum plotters draw on paper wrapped around a cylinder. Flat-bed plotters draw on paper fixed to a flat surface. And electro-static plotters use electrostatic means for forming the image. Electrostatic plotters, however, produce the final image in a

Figure 4.5 A modern high-speed belt plotter. (Courtesy of Cal-Comp Ltd.)

totally different way from the other types. Instead of moving a pen in a semi-random, zig-zag fashion, the displayed co-ordinates are delivered to the plotter stored on a reel of magnetic tape. They are then sorted by a small computer sys-tem perhaps in ascending X-coordinate sequence (i.e., points with a smaller X value are placed before larger values, etc.) and they are scanned and printed by a long electrostatic print-ing head with a resolution of approximately 200 dots per inch. Thus the picture appears from the system on a continuous roll of paper. Figure 4.6 illustrates an electrostatic plotter manufac-tured by CalComp Ltd.

Non-electrostatic plotters create pictures composed of lines; and line thickness and colour can only be achieved by altering

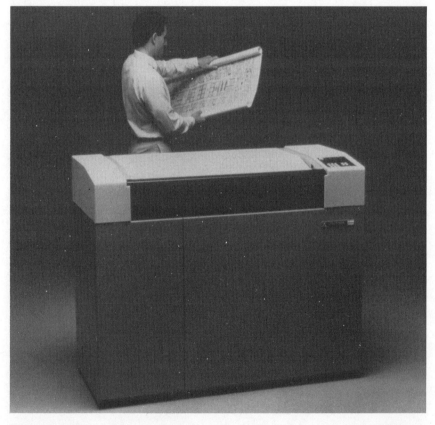

Figure 4.6 A high-resolution electrostatic plotter. (Courtesy of CalComp Ltd.)

the current biro or pen. To cater for these design requirements, some are equipped with eight or more selectable pens. Perhaps the reader can already see that it would be quite difficult to use these devices to form large blocks of colour on artwork and also graduated colours. The direct output of coloured images is possible but a discussion of these devices has been left until Chapter 12.

4.3 Graphic display terminals

Early computer terminals were very primitive devices compared to the sophisticated display terminals available today. They were slow and noisy and painstakingly hammered out their information upon endless rolls of paper that inevitably ended up in a waste-paper bin. Modern computer terminals exploit the advances made in television screen technology which are mass-produced very cheaply.

Now, a monochrome television picture is made up from a matrix of dots, called pixels, in the form of 576 lines by 768 pixels; in total almost 500,000 pixels. This can be used to display text, so long as the text is also constructed from a pattern of points; therefore, in a visual display unit (VDU), electronic character generators automatically produce fonts in this way.

If the same screen is used to display images constructed from lines, they must also decompose into pixels. To achieve this, the terminal is equipped with sufficient memory in the form of silicon chips, which are scanned electronically every 1/25th of a second. If the memory chips store nothing but binary '0', then the screen remains blank; but if coordinates are sent to the terminal, extra electronics set certain pixels to binary '1' in line formation, and as this memory is being scanned twenty-five times every second, the picture is observed being traced as fast as the terminal can function. This type of terminal is very popular in computer graphic systems and an example is shown in Figure 4.7.

If the user requires to move the displayed picture in some way—perhaps in the form of panning, zooming, rotation or animation—the current picture must be erased before a replacement is displayed. The screen erasure is achieved by

Figure 4.7 This graphic display terminal is capable of displaying 24 rows of 80-column text, or graphics to a resolution of 512 × 512.

cancelling the binary signal stored within the display's memory, and if the new coordinates can be supplied and displayed within 1/25th of a second, real-time movements can be achieved. Naturally, the more coordinates displayed the more difficult it becomes to maintain the display at twenty-five times a second; therefore, the image will hesitate as it is refreshed.

4.4 Vector display devices

Another important type of display device is called a vector display, as it maintains its image by continuously refreshing the screen by drawing the lines (vectors) from start to end. The display terminal is equipped with memory capable of storing the coordinates comprising the image. As the display file is scanned, the electron beam—which creates any television picture—is moved accordingly over the screen's surface forming the image. When the file is processed it is rescanned automatically, and if the list of coordinates does not exceed a certain limit, the system is able to refresh the screen without flickering. This method of display is again very useful for real-time movements, because once the display file has been stored within the terminal, panning, zooming and rotational operations can be achieved at high-speed using special hardware to undertake the arithmetic operations. A vector display device is illustrated in Figure 4.8.

Figure 4.8 This vector display device maintains an image by repeatedly scanning internally stored vectors (lines). (Courtesy of Imlac International Ltd.)

4.5 Other graphic devices

Apart from the conventional display devices described above, computer graphic systems depend on other devices that simplify the delicate interface between user and machine. These have acquired exotic names such as 'joystick', 'tracker-ball', 'mouse', etc.

The joystick

The joystick is a convenient device for positioning cross-hairs displayed upon a graphic screen, perhaps in the context of menu selection. This device enables a user to select from a menu of commands displayed upon a terminal a specific command which can be undertaken by the system.

Basically it consists of a short control stick constrained by springs, and when pressure is applied in any direction, internal electronics code the movement which can be interpreted by a computer program. A joystick is illustrated in Figure 4.9.

Figure 4.9 A joystick.

The trackerball

In some circumstances a trackerball is preferred to a joystick in controlling cross-hairs displayed upon a graphic screen. Some people claim that they prefer the response to moving a trackerball to that from operating a joystick. It is operated by rolling a heavy ball in any desired direction and, again, internal electronics encode its movement.

Touch screens

Another simple mechanism permitting users to communicate with a computer is a touch screen. Initially, the computer program displays a choice of actions acceptable to the program. The user, by pointing to the command displayed upon a screen, interrupts a pattern of horizontal and vertical infra-red beams protecting the screen's surface. Suitable electronic equipment is then capable of detecting the position identified by the user's finger and transmits the selected position to the program.

Thumb-wheels

One of the first mechanisms for improving man-machine communication was via two cross-hairs displayed upon a graphics screen. On the terminal were mounted two wheels, called thumb-wheels, which controlled the horizontal and vertical positions of the cross-hairs. The point of intersection of the two cross-hairs could be controlled by the two thumb-wheels, enabling the user to select a command from a menu selection. Figure 4.10 illustrates a display screen equipped with a cursor controlled by thumb-wheels.

Mouse

The mouse is proving to be an extremely popular device especially on microcomputers such as the Macintosh. It consists of a hand-held device which is moved over any surface, and as its internal wheels turn, its movement is encoded electronically and transmitted to the computer. Again it is very useful in menu selection activities.

Cursor keys

Graphic screens equipped with a cursor or cross-hairs sometimes have an associated keyboard which contains eight keys controlling it. The keys enable the cursor to be moved left, right, up, down and diagonally.

Figure 4.10 Thumbwheels are used for controlling the position of a graphic screen's cross-hairs.

Light pen

A light pen is used in conjunction with a graphics terminal, and permits the user to point and touch the screen as a response to some command. Within the pen is encapsulated a small photo-sensitive cell, which transmits back to the terminal a small signal when it is energised by the scanning raster. Because the video raster is precisely timed by the scanning electronics, it is possible for the system to compute the screen position referenced by the user. In the past, it has been criticised for placing a strain upon the user, who must operate with an outstretched arm, relatively close to a video screen, but in spite of this it is still very popular.

4.6 Summary

The success of any computer system depends greatly upon the ease with which users can use it. Currently, we rely upon a mixture of input and output devices to ease the communication between man and machine, and in the area of computer graphics these peripherals consist of:

- the digitizer to create Cartesian coordinates and help address a graphics screen;

- the graph plotter which turns coordinates back into line drawings;

- graphic display devices which also display coordinates as line drawings;

- and various other devices such as: the joystick, trackerball, thumb-wheels, cursor keys, touch screen and light pen.

5 2D monochrome applications

'There are no such things as applied sciences, only applications of science.'

Louis Pasteur

We have now examined the basic elements comprising any computer graphics system: the central computer unit with its operating system and disk; various graphic peripherals; and that ever vital software. Perhaps now we can consider how such a system can be usefully applied. Remember that there is no reason for using such sophisticated technology unless there are some obvious real benefits. A computer system ought to be able to save time, improve accuracy, simplify the storage of images and so allow us to undertake more complex and sophisticated design activities; but if a computer is being installed just for the sake of computerising, expect trouble!

In Chapter 3, I suggested the range of graphic facilities that might be needed to aid a design process. Now we have discovered that certain two-dimensional facilities are possible and, in monochrome, let us identify some design activities that might benefit from computerisation.

2D drafting systems

Computer graphic systems are beginning to play a very important role in drafting processes where large numbers of drawings have to be prepared, modified, duplicated and maintained, for example: engineering drafting systems, large-scale integrated circuit design, architectural drafting, and electrical wiring diagrams. All of these activities basically share the same requirements, i.e. the ability to input rapidly and accurately 2D line drawings; preview the whole or parts upon a display screen; correct and continuously extend the image; output upon paper or micro-fiche any number of copies; and store large volumes of images digitally, compactly and securely within the system. The system is shown diagramatically in Figure 5.1, and Figure 5.2 illustrates an actual system manufactured by CalComp Ltd.

It is important to appreciate that users of these systems need to know nothing about programming, for the software supplied with the system incorporates all of the drafting facilities the manufacturer has anticipated for their customers. These are commonly called turnkey systems, as the user has to do nothing more than turn a key to activate the system, but that is not to say that anyone can use them without some sort of training. Many of these systems offer incredible drafting facilities and features never before conventionally available, such as: zooming, panning, automatic curve fitting, dimensioning in any units, computation of area and circumference, scaling, stretching, etc., all of which are activated by zones on one or more menus. It takes time to become familiar with these menus, and master all the facilities available; nevertheless, it is incredible to see the speed with which an experienced user can create images. Figure 5.3 illustrates an example of a drawing created and plotted by the MEDUSA system.

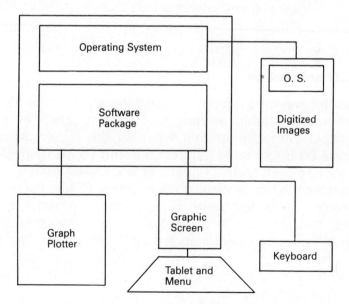

Figure 5.1 These are the basic elements required for an interactive 2D drafting system.

Figure 5.2 A modern CAD workstation. (Courtesy of Applied Research of Cambridge Ltd.)

5.2 2D animation

Successful animation depends upon the ability to create long sequences of related images, and display them at a rate compatible with film or television. In the United Kingdom these are 24 fps (frames per second) and 25 fps respectively. Even for one minute, this implies at least 1,440 images.

To reduce the tremendous drawing load on skilled animators, it is conventional for them to produce a sequence of 'key frames' comprising the animation, which are then linked together by another person called an 'inbetweener'. In certain cases, the inbetweening is a mechanical and predictable process which can be computerised, and is successfully used by some animation studios.

The inbetweening program functions as follows. Consider the two key contours 'A' and 'B' shown in Figure 5.4. If these

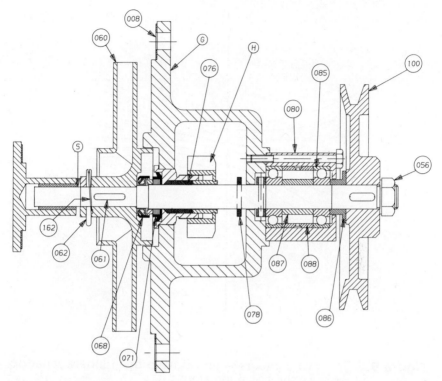

Figure 5.3 A 2D drawing produced by the MEDUSA CAD system.

are digitized and stored within a computer as two lists of coordinates, it is possible to compute any inbetween frame using the following formula:

$$X_{inbetween} = X_A + (X_B - X_A) * P$$

$$Y_{inbetween} = Y_A + (Y_B - Y_A) * P$$

where X_A, Y_A and X_B, Y_B are corresponding points on the two contours, and P is a number which varies between 0.0 and 1.0. When P equals 0.0:

$$X_{inbetween} = X_A \text{ and}$$

$$Y_{inbetween} = Y_A$$

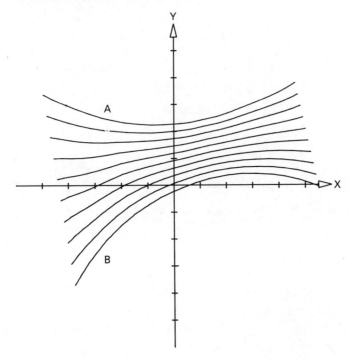

Figure 5.4 The two contours A and B have been inbetweened to produce the transition stages.

and when $P = 1.0$:

$$X_{inbetween} = X_B \text{ and}$$

$$Y_{inbetween} = Y_B.$$

Consequently, when $P = 0.5$:

$$X_{inbetween} = (X_A + X_B)/2 \quad \text{and}$$

$$Y_{inbetween} = (Y_A + Y_B)/2 \; .$$

This particular explanation assumes that both contours have the same number of points.

Obviously this formula can also be incorporated within a computer program which can display the inbetween contour for different values of P. Say, for example, the inbetweening was required over eleven images, the program has to alter the value of P from 0.0 to 1.0 in eleven stages. So P will start at 0.0 and then increment in steps of 0.1 until it reaches 1.0. This is a trivial task for any computer. But what of the animation? What will it look like? Will it appear smooth? Only a line test will resolve these questions, and some computers are capable of displaying the animation in real time, making intermediate filming unnecessary.

One consequence of this inbetweening formula is that the image will appear smooth, but starts and finishes abruptly. To smooth out the frames at the start and end, all that is needed is to arrange for the value of P to change slowly to begin with, progress linearly, and then once more change slowly until it reaches 1.0. This variation in the value of P is shown graphically in Figure 5.5, and is equivalent to the animator's skill of fairing or cushioning movements.

It is possible to devise programs which are capable of in-betweening contours of unequal numbers of points, and also unequal numbers of contours; but with the latter condition it can be difficult to predict the inbetweened images as it must

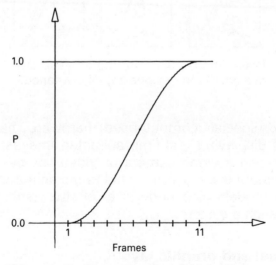

Figure 5.5 This graph illustrates the fairing that can be incorporated within computer programs to improve animated movements.

result in some form of contour disintegration. Figure 5.6 shows an animated sequence of two unrelated scenes being in-betweened.

Obviously, it is possible to devise computer programs which are capable of manipulating two-dimensional images, and provide a style of animation perhaps impossible using conventional animation techniques. But as we shall see shortly, computer graphics creates a world of its own when it manipulates three-dimensional images.

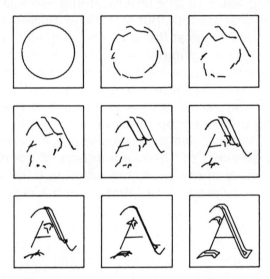

Figure 5.6 These images illustrate the breakup that occurs when two unrelated designs are inbetweened.

Recently, special computerised hardware has evolved capable of displaying real-time animated images, which are input either via a video camera or video source. This solid-state equipment is a marvellous aid to the animation industry, and some models also undertake inbetweening. Figure 5.7 illustrates such a system.

5.3 Textual and graphic layout

Johannes Gutenberg built his first printing press about 1450, and within fifty years the world's printing industry had pro-

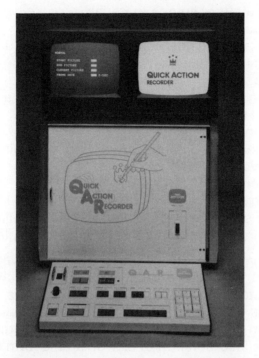

Figure 5.7 This real-time, solid-state system can animate mono-chrome images input from a video source.

duced approximately 9 million books. Five hundred years later sections of our twentieth-century newspaper industry still employed the technology of setting in hot lead, simply because nothing better had been discovered. But today, digital technology is dramatically revolutionising these procedures.

As an example, the original draft for this book was hand-written, and then input into a BBC microcomputer using a word processing program. The word processor facility permitted the author to continuously revise the manuscript, altering spelling, punctuation and the juxtaposition of para-graphs. Final pages could be previewed, and even camera-ready copy could have been output via a daisy-wheel printer.

Commercial systems exceed the author's equipment by several orders of magnitude in terms of facilities; they include features such as:

- the direct input of source material;
- telecommunication links;
- automatic spelling checks against an internal dictionary;
- automatic hyphenation;
- automatic transmission from one language to another (subject to human intervention on idiomatic and complex contextual cases);
- justification;
- multiple fonts of different sizes, and symbols for mathematics, science, music and logos;
- on-line storage;
- interactive modification of internal fonts;
- electronic scanning to output upon paper or film;
- laser scanning to output upon film, paper or plate.

Naturally, some of these systems are expensive, and many only relevant to the newspaper industry, but with the availability of systems based upon microcomputers, their cost-effectiveness will overcome any industrial inertia.

One major stumbling block for digital typesetting systems has been the incorporation of artwork in the form of diagrams and photographs. But, currently, great technological strides are being made in this area and, already, systems exist capable of interactively editing colour pictures and text. The future then, appears very exciting for the printing industry because, although some aspects of our lives are becoming paperless, documents, brochures and books still do not have a serious silicon-based rival.

5.4 Summary

The whole point of computerising any manual process is to reap some benefit in the form of cost, time, efficiency, conditions, etc. Already, computers have proven their worth within a number of graphic-based industries, and in the previous sections the following points were raised:

- Very powerful 2D drafting systems are available to support engineering, mapping, architecture and the electronics industries.

- Turnkey systems incorporate all the necessary programming to undertake a user's needs.

- In spite of these specialist systems not requiring programming, users still require extensive training.

- Animation is an obvious application for computers, as computer programs can be designed to assist in the inbetweening of key frames.

- The natural animator's skill of fairing or cushioning can be incorporated within programs.

- Hardware exists for line testing and inbetweening.

- The current revolution in information technology will have a tremendous impact upon the printing industries during the next decade, as computer-based systems evolve permitting the manipulation of text and high-resolution colour graphics.

6 Colour in computer graphic systems

'What soul was his, when from the naked top
Of some bold headland, he beheld the sun
Rise up, and bathe the world in light!'

William Wordsworth

I have deliberately delayed a description of the way colour is handled in computer graphic systems, as the subject is relatively large and demands special attention if the important aspects are to be treated in some detail. Colour theory itself is a complex science, which has been investigated and documented over the last four hundred years; and as the ideas employed in computer graphic systems depend upon classical principles, I will briefly summarise those events and theories which are pertinent to the current usage of colour.

6.1 Light and colour

Two practical ways of describing our universe are with the use of words or with mathematical symbols; both are necessary and both are useful. Perhaps only a paragraph or two is required to explain the formation of a planetary system to a lay person, but a mathematical description would require reams of paper and even then be totally incomprehensible to the non-mathematician. So when one considers an esoteric subject like electromagnetic radiation, the choice between words and mathematics is decided by the audience, and as you, the reader, are probably connected with the design world, rather than physics, the choice is obvious. So the following description relies heavily upon words, some of which have a physical meaning and others are the result of words being associated with new mathematical concepts.

So to start with, what is meant by light? It is a natural part of our universe and belongs to the spectrum of electromagnetic radiation. This radiation encompasses: X-rays, micro-waves (cooking), television waves, radio waves, infra-red (heat), light waves (vision), ultra-violet waves (sun-tanning), etc., and they all travel at approximately 186,000 miles per second in empty space. The one characteristic that distinguishes one type of radiation from another is the wave-length. This is a physical measurement and represents the distance between two corresponding points in the undulations that occur electromagnetically. Figure 6.1 illustrates this graphically. Television waves are approximately 5.0 metres long whilst X-rays are 0.0000000001 metres, very short indeed.

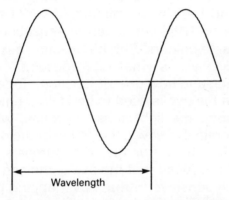

Figure 6.1 Electromagnetic radiation can be described graphically as sinusoidal undulations. The associated wavelength represents the distance between two corresponding points on this curve.

Our eyes have evolved with a sensitivity to part of this spectrum between the wave length limits of approximately 0.0000004 metres to 0.0000007 metres or 400 nm (nanometres) to 700 nm. It just so happens that the longer wavelengths, i.e. those around 700 nm, produce a red sensation in our brains whilst the shortest, around 400 nm, create a deep violet sensation. Notice that colour is an invention of our nervous system rather than being a physical part of the external world.

The next natural question to raise is, what colour sensations are produced as the wave-length is changed from 700 nm to 400 nm? The answer to this is found in rainbows which optically spread this portion of the electromagnetic spectrum.

Prisms also perform the same action by bending short wavelengths more than longer ones. Isaac Newton demonstrated the effect of taking a beam of white light and passing it through a prism which created the rainbow banding of colours—red, orange, yellow, green, blue and violet. This implied that white light was nothing more than the brain's response to receiving the eye's signals to a mixture of all the wave-lengths.

So pure colour appears to be controlled by the wave-length of radiation; but just like sound it is very rarely pure, there always tends to be a large mixture of various wave-lengths which provide us with the apparent sensation of an infinite range of available colours. But the question asked, for at least two thousand years, is what role does the eye play in the process of vision and how does it function? Today, we all know that the lens in the eye is used to bend light entering the pupil focussing it upon the light sensitive retina, which transmits signals to the brain. However, the action of the retina proved to be the stumbling block for many researchers, until Thomas Young in 1802 proposed that the eye contained three types of receptors, each sensitive to three overlapping portions of the visible spectrum. This is shown in Figure 6.2. Basically, the principle colour portions sampled by the eye represent the red, green and blue parts of the spectrum.

Helmholtz extended Young's hypothesis and it is now known as the Young–Helmholtz trichromatic theory. Fortunately,

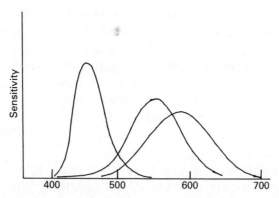

Figure 6.2 The three response curves of sensitivity exhibited by the human eye.

recent experiments have confirmed these basic ideas, but active research is still in progress concerning how the brain interprets the eye's signals to produce the sensation of colour.

Many experiments have been performed showing that any colour sensation can be created by mixing together different amounts of red, green and blue light. In fact, Dr Land (Polaroid Corp.) has conducted some very interesting experiments, where only two primary colours are necessary to create a wide range of realistic colour sensations.

6.2 Frame stores

This basic sampling action of the eye is exploited by television technology, which translates the colour information received by a video camera into three primary colours: red, green and blue. This colour information is encoded electronically and transmitted. At the receiving end, the signal is decoded and the primary colour information extracted electronically. These separate signals are used to stimulate a matrix of red, green and blue phosphor dots which ultimately form the television's picture. Because the dots are close together, the eye effectively integrates the separate colours to generate different colour sensations. The next time you have the opportunity, try placing upon a working television screen several droplets of water, and observe the screen's colour construction.

This ability to reduce a colour screen to three colour separations: red, green and blue is also exploited within computer graphic peripherals. For example, if every pixel on a graphic display screen has three bits of memory to store the colour detail (R = red, G = green, B = blue), the following binary codes would produce these colours:

RGB	
000	black
001	blue
010	green
011	cyan
100	red
101	magenta
110	yellow
111	white

which is why many micros and terminals only display eight colours.

If a larger variety of colours were required, more memory has to be allocated to each pixel. If, for example, a byte is allocated to each pixel, there will be 256 possible codes, ranging from 00000000 to 11111111. But the specific colours allocated to each code are stored in a system component called a look-up table which is prepared and selected by the user. It could be that the code 00000111 (representing 7)—which references the seventh position of the look-up table, and identifies the levels of red, green and blue to use—stores red = 255, green = 255 and blue = 20, which would appear as a slightly desaturated yellow.

This referencing is shown diagrammatically in Figure 6.3. If the look-up table is itself constructed from whole bytes, one for each primary colour, it implies that each table entry is described in terms of one of 256 levels of red, green and blue.

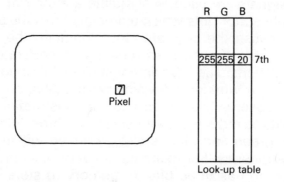

Figure 6.3 If a pixel's value is 7, its colour codes will be found in the 7th position of the look-up table. In this example: red = 255, green = 255, and blue = 20.

Hence, any colour is specified in terms of 0 to 255 levels of red, green and blue, which in total supplies approximately 16.7 million colours (256 × 256 × 256). Because the byte can only store 256 codes, there are colour display devices capable of displaying 16.7 million colours, but only 256 simultaneously.

To extend the range of colours even further requires more memory allocated to a pixel, but the memory size and associated electronics often demands for it to be separated from the terminal. The resulting piece of equipment is called a frame store, a photograph of which is shown in Figure 6.4. It is called a frame store because it stores one television image, i.e. a frame, in digital code.

The best way to envisage a true colour frame store is as three planes of computer memory which individually hold the three colour separations. These planes of memory constructed from bytes, are electronically scanned every 1/25th of a second and supply the colour signals eventually interpreted by a colour monitor. The look-up table is still used as it provides extra flexibility in changing colours. Figure 6.5 illustrates a diagramatic representation of a frame store.

Normally the look-up tables hold values ranging from 000 to 255, so that the values held in the memory planes generate the same number after being indexed by the tables. For example, if a memory value had been 36, the 36th position of

Figure 6.4 This frame store consists of 3 MBytes of memory, and is capable of storing images to a resolution of 1,024 × 1,024 in 16.7 million colours.

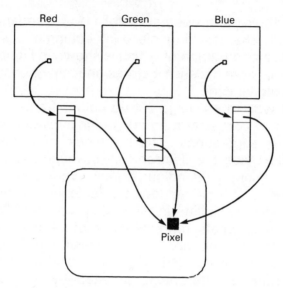

Figure 6.5 A 24-bit deep (3 byte) frame store can hold three numbers representing the levels of red, green and blue for each pixel. Look-up tables can still be employed to alter the final colour levels, as shown.

the look-up table would also store 36, thus very little is achieved; but if the look-up table entries were altered, there would be an instant change in the colours displayed upon the monitor. This technique is called false colouring and is used in the image processing of satellite and medical imaging systems, but is also exploited in some television graphic effects.

Just imagine the flexibility this could give a designer of textiles, whereby a simple interactive command with a frame store could instantly alter colour combinations displayed upon a monitor.

So a frame store, then, is nothing more than a block of memory interfacing the computer to a colour monitor.

6.3 Colour description

Now that we have discovered a device for holding colour pictures, we need an effective procedure for handling colour within computer programs, and if the problem is not immediately obvious, just consider the difficulty in determining the levels of red, green and blue to produce a salmon pink or slate blue. Fortunately the problem had been investigated by several people long before a solution was needed within computer graphics. Munsell's work, in particular, has been very useful for computer programmers, for in 1915 he published his *Atlas of the Munsell Colour System* in which he printed ordered sequences of colours arranged in terms of three parameters: hue (dominant wavelength), value (lightness or brightness), and saturation (strength or purity). These parameters enabled colours to be represented three-dimensionally in the form of a distorted sphere, referred to as the Munsell colour tree.

The five basic hues (red, yellow, green, blue and purple) and the intermediate colours (yellow-red, green-yellow, blue-green, purple-blue and red-purple) are arranged around the central vertical axis. The further a colour is from this axis, the more saturated it becomes; thus colours approaching the centre of the volume slowly lose their colour information and reduce to a grey.

The vertical position of any colour within the Munsell tree controls its brightness. This organisation implies that the surface of the volume contains the saturated colours starting with black at the bottom, finishing with bright white at the top.

After Munsell's death, a new edition of the atlas was published renamed *The Munsell Book of Colour* (1929). This included modifications in the way brightness was measured in the vertical scale. Initially, Munsell had created ten equal divisions on a square root scale of reflectance to ensure that brightness changes were reasonably well spaced; and although this approximated to the psychological appreciation of brightness, the revised edition was even more acceptable.

This model, then, represents the eye's subjective sensitivity to colour, and because of its asymmetry it would be extremely difficult to mimic in computer programs. What is needed is an objective way of controlling colour description that is accurate and simple to implement.

6.4 The RGB colour cube

Consider then the possibility of describing colour, like Munsell, geometrically, but starting with the premise that any colour can be composed of different amounts of red, green and blue—which is not entirely true, but good enough. A set of 3D Cartesian axes can be constructed along the lines shown in Figure 6.6. Thus, any pure red colour can only exist precisely upon the red axis, and the further it is from the origin, the brighter it becomes. This applies equally for the pure green and blue colours.

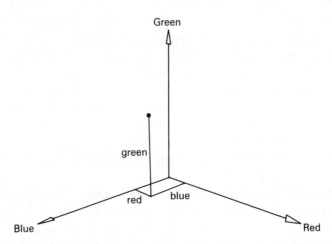

Figure 6.6 A 3D Cartesian set of axes can be used to assist in the description of colour, such that any point within this space is defined in terms of its: red, green, and blue components.

Now also assume that the eye's bias towards red and green is accounted for elsewhere in the system. Then equal amounts of red, green and blue create a white sensation depending upon the magnitude. This implies that saturated colours, i.e. colours without any white component, are composed from any two of the original primaries. Therefore, in the plane containing the red and green axes one will find the saturated colours ranging from red, orange, yellow and green of different brightnesses. Similarly, the plane containing green and blue contains cyan, and the plane containing blue and red contains magenta. These planes are shown in the form of a cube in Figure 6.7, and establishes a symmetric volume that is easily analysed.

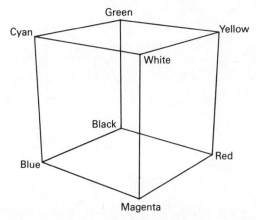

Figure 6.7 The colour cube identifies the relationships between the primary colours and their mixtures.

The next step in this analysis is to construct within this volume a mechanism for referencing hue, saturation and brightness. This is not too difficult if one already knows the answer. So here is the explanation.

If one joins the point of total blackness to total whiteness, the connecting line contains the range of greys from black to white, which are totally desaturated colours. Consequently, the further a colour is from this line, the greater its purity or saturation; and the nearer it is to white, the brighter it becomes. Figure 6.8 illustrates this geometric relationship. But how is hue controlled? A convenient way of visualising hue is to consider the colour cube when viewed from the white corner looking down towards black as shown in Figure 6.9. The hue of a point *C* can be uniquely defined in terms of an angle it forms with the red axis and a line joining *C* to the line of greys.

So there we are. Hue can be represented by an angle, saturation by a number representing the ratio of the colour's distance from the grey line, and brightness by the relative distance between black and white.

This colour cube forms the basis of encoding techniques employed in video systems; in fact when levels of red, green and blue are encoded, the eye's sensitivity which reaches a maximum around 550 nm is taken into account, then the broadcast signal for luminance, which controls a picture's

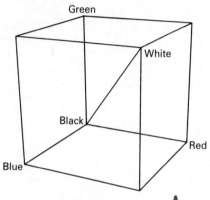

Figure 6.8 Moving along the line from black to white increases brightness, whilst moving away from the line increases saturation.

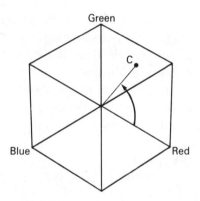

Figure 6.9 Here we see the colour cube viewed from the white corner looking towards black. The hue of colour C can be described by an angle relative to the red axis.

brightness, is made up from approximately 30 per cent red, 60 per cent green and 10 per cent blue.

But this explanation is still not complete, for the hue, saturation and value model frequently employed in computer graphic programs is derived from the colour cube model. Returning once more to the colour cube view shown in Figure 6.9 one sees a hexagonal spread of colour which is said to have the same value. But another hexagonal spread of colour can be produced by considering a half-size cube within the same space, as shown in Figure 6.10. In fact there are infinite number of effective hexagons that reduce in size as the value is reduced.

Rather than attempting to visualise the hexagons on the cubes, it is much easier to organise them as cross-sections

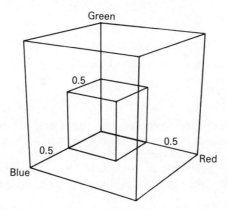

Figure 6.10 This unit colour cube also contains a smaller cube the surface of which forms a hexagonal area of value = 0.5.

through a hexcone as shown in Figure 6.11, which is both simple to visualise and simple to analyse geometrically, but more importantly it is quite close to the way designers manipulate colours.

Using this model, it is a semi-trivial task to design a computer program capable of translating levels of hue, saturation and value into levels of red, green and blue, and vice versa.

The actual specification of a colour can now be made numerically in the form of three numbers, perhaps all between the range 0.0 to 1.0. For example, a hue of 0.0 represents red, whilst 0.333 is equivalent to green and 0.666 is equivalent to blue; as the hue increases towards 1.0 so the colour returns to red. This is called the hue circle.

For any particular hue, the amount of white light included, is controlled by the saturation level; a saturation value of 0.0 is conventionally assumed to indicate a grey, whilst a value of 1.0

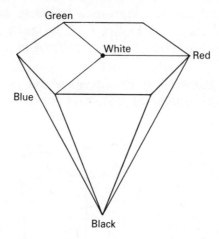

Figure 6.11 A simple hexcone can be used to relate the parameters: hue, saturation and value. Hue is controlled by
a horizontal angle relative to the red axis; saturation is
the percentage distance from the black–white axis;
and value is the height from black to white.

implies totally saturated. Accordingly, value is also specified
by a number between 0.0 and 1.0. Table 6.1 illustrates values of
hue, saturation and value and the encoded colour.

An interesting feature of the hexcone model is that it gives
an immediate access to complementary colours. The comple-
ment being diametrically opposite the chosen colour implies
that the difference in hues must be 0.5. As an example, the

Table 6.1

Hue	Saturation	Value	Colour	
0.0	1.0	1.0	bright	red
1.0	1.0	1.0	bright	red
-	0.0	1.0	bright	white
-	0.0	0.0	black	
-	0.0	0.5	mid	grey
0.166	1.0	1.0	bright	yellow
0.500	1.0	1.0	bright	cyan
0.833	1.0	1.0	bright	magenta

component of pure blue (hue = 0.6666) must be yellow (hue = 0.1666). But apart from this, the hue, saturation, value model is important when colour changes have to be made in a program, where either the hue, saturation or value must remain constant and the other two change.

6.5 Summary

As we have seen, colour is quite a complex subject, and yet I have only touched upon some of the simple ideas. Nevertheless, they are sufficient for us to understand the way colour is employed in computer graphic systems. Here, then, are the points to remember:

- The human eye is sensitive to part of the electromagnetic spectrum which is called light; the wavelengths are between 700 nm and 400 nm.

- The brain creates a red sensation at 700 nm and as the wavelength shortens produces orange, yellow, green, cyan and blue, down to violet at 400 nm. Other colours depend upon the mixture of different wavelengths reflected or transmitted by an object.

- The trichromatic theory postulated by Young states that the eye samples incoming light over three portions of the spectrum concerning red, green and blue, and that the majority of colours can be produced by mixing different levels of red, green, and blue light.

- Colour display terminals create pictures by stimulating a matrix of red, green and blue dots, which are integrated by the eye creating a unique colour sensation.

- A frame store is a peripheral capable of maintaining within memory colour information for each pixel displayed. It also employs a component called a look-up table, which permits the instantaneous manipulation of red, green and blue levels.

- The RGB colour cube enables colours to be defined geometrically using a Cartesian description.

● Colour specification and manipulation within computer graphics is simplified by employing the parameters: hue, saturation and value; these also can be described geometrically using a hexcone.

● Programs are available which convert values of hue, saturation and value into levels of red, green, and blue, and vice versa.

Plate 1 'Collage'—first-year group from four-year BA (Hons.) Graphic Design, Middlesex Polytechnic, 1985.

Plate II 'Statue of Liberty'—modelled and shaded by Keith Waters, Graphic Design student at Middlesex Polytechnic, 1985.

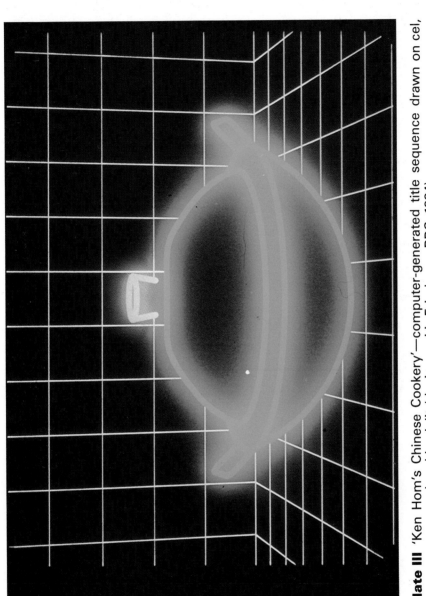

Plate III 'Ken Hom's Chinese Cookery'—computer-generated title sequence drawn on cel, reversed and back lit (designer: Liz Friedman, BBC, 1984).

Plate IV 'Open Space'—computer-generated title sequence drawn on cel, back-painted, top lit and back lit (designer: Liz Friedman, BBC, 1984).

Plate V A flat shaded image of an object illuminated with two light sources.

Plate VI Two toroids rendered with flat and smooth shading using two light sources.

Plate VII A Phong shaded scene with four light sources.

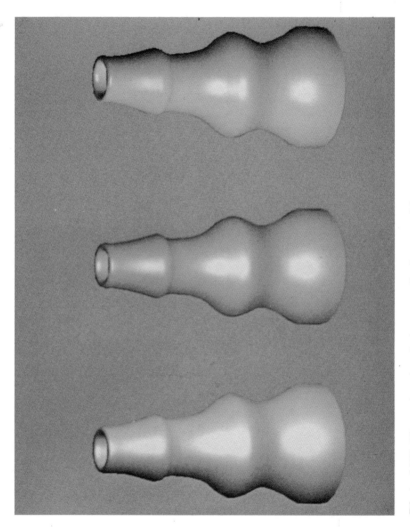

Plate VIII Three levels of gloss applied to an object.

7 2D application of frame stores

'A little amateur painting in water-colours shows the innocent and quiet mind.'

Robert Louis Stevenson

The frame store is such a flexible device that it is worth considering separately its use in colour painting systems. Already, painting systems are now available upon the humble micro as well as the sophisticated turnkey systems manufactured by RGB Computers, Logica and Quantel.

7.1 Paint systems

Logically, a painting system enables a user to 'spray' numbers into a frame store using a computer, which is driven by suitable software controlled interactively by a tablet. This is shown diagramatically in Figure 7.1. The painting software enables the user to select colours from a simple palette displayed upon the screen. These can be mixed together to create different shades and stored alongside existing colours. As a stylus is moved over a tablet's surface the corresponding pixels of the frame store are set to a look-up table entry holding the levels of red, green and blue, corresponding to the colour, but simultaneously the user sees in real-time the coloured design displayed upon a monitor. It is essential that the system is capable of following the rapid movements made by the stylus, otherwise a sense of inertia is felt by the user who is forced to adjust to an unnatural speed.

Quantel's Paint Box system, shown in Figure 7.2 provides the user with:

- different brush sizes which effectively spread the numbers over more pixels within the frame store;
- four paint modes (water-colour, oils, gouache and air brush);
- stencils;

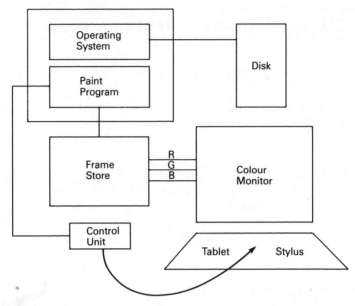

Figure 7.1 A diagram of a paint system employing a digital frame store.

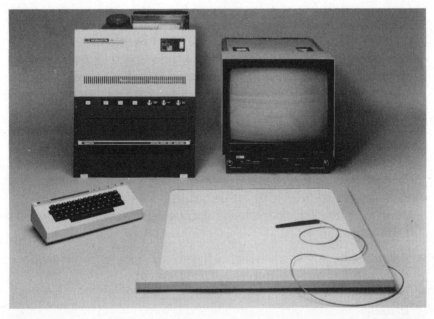

Figure 7.2 Quantel's Paint Box System. (Courtesy of Quantel Ltd.)

- text;
- animation;
- two-times zoom, and picture rotation;
- video input and output of images, and many more features.

One superb feature of Quantel's system is the pressure-sensitive stylus, which permits the user to control colour opacity by varying the pressure applied to it. A light pressure creates a delicate wash of transparent colour, where the current frame store colour is allowed to dominate that being entered, whilst a firm pressure ensures that previously applied colour is masked by the stylus colour. Plate 1 shows an image produced by a digital painting system.

Painting systems are widely employed in the television industry, where they are used to prepare a wide variety of artwork required for news and current-affairs programmes. They are also proving very fashionable in the preparation of colour slides as they enable sophisticated graphic effects to be employed quickly, and are cost effective compared with conventional methods.

7.2 Summary

The underlying idea behind paint systems is very simple, and yet some very sophisticated hardware and software is required to implement broadcast-quality systems. The following aspects are worth noting:

- Paint systems require a digital frame store to maintain the colour information.

- Clever software must be capable of imitating the mixing and application of colour.

- Very fast processors are needed to ensure the system responds rapidly to a user's actions.

- Paint systems must have some digital library system for storing images.

8 3D computer graphics

'Nothing puzzles me more than time and space; and yet nothing troubles me less, as I never think about them.'

Charles Lamb

Personally, I find the three-dimensional aspects of computer graphic systems the most exciting, as one has the ability to construct impossible worlds, produce improbable objects and undertake animated journeys over fantastic terrains. Fortunately, it is not too difficult to understand, so long as we take it in stages.

First of all, it is essential to comprehend how three-dimensional descriptions of space are made and then how perspective views of objects are produced by a program. By using a frame store, we can examine the techniques required for colouring and shading computer-generated scenes; and finally, examine how such systems can be usefully employed. So to start let us return to the ideas of Cartesian description.

8.1 3D Cartesian coordinates

In flat two-dimensional space, two coordinates are necessary to identify a point relative to an origin, therefore, one would expect three coordinates to be needed to fix a point in three-dimensional space. Figure 8.1 illustrates how this notation functions for a point P which has coordinates (X, Y, Z).

This type of space is called right-handed space, as one can take one's right hand and place the thumb along the X-axis, the first finger along the Y-axis and the middle finger along the Z-axis. Left-handed space requires a reversal of the Z-axis, but is not often used in computer graphic programs. So to store a straight line in three dimensions requires six numbers, i.e. the points (vertices) at each end, $2 \times 3 = 6$.

A three-dimensional object can then be constructed from lines. However, these are called 'edges', as they represent a boundary between two sides. The definition of objects is very

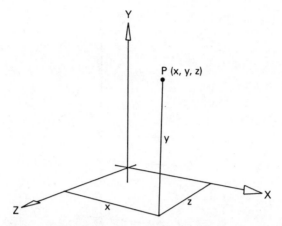

Figure 8.1 This set of 3D axes is used to locate points in space. The point P is defined by the coordinates (x, y, z).

important in computer graphics, because without a rigorous construction it might prove very difficult to manipulate and shade within a computer program.

To illustrate this idea of construction, consider how the cube shown in Figure 8.2 could be stored. If every side has a length of 1 the coordinates would be as in Table 8.2.

But a cube is constructed from six facets (sides), each formed from four edges; so one possible definition could be in the form of facets which in turn consist of edges. Table 8.3 illustrates this relationship.

Table 8.2

Vertex	X	Y	Z
1	0	0	0
2	0	0	1
3	0	1	1
4	0	1	0
5	1	0	0
6	1	0	1
7	1	1	1
8	1	1	0

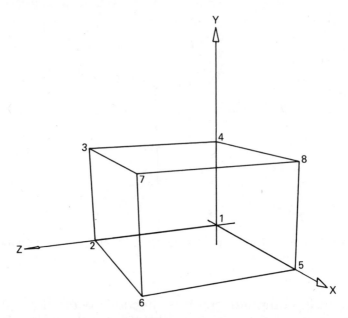

Figure 8.2 A cube could be stored by identifying each vertex with coordinates, and then organising a data structure to describe each side.

The numbers in the vertex columns refer to Table 8.2 containing the original vertices.

Now this type of definition enables a program access to any vertex, edge or side, which implies that the whole, or any part of the object can be drawn by a computer. When a program is used to shade the object according to the natural laws of illumination, further information is required, such as the orientation of sides, and the sides shared by any vertex.

The modelling of three-dimensional objects is an extremely important aspect of computer graphics, and I will examine modelling techniques in Chapter 9. However, for the time being just assume that any stored object is in the form of coordinates organised in groups to create facets. This internal organisation is called a data structure.

8.2 The manipulation of 3D coordinates

Earlier (in Section 3.3), I illustrated how a computer can manipulate coordinates to control size, position, rotation and create

Table 8.3

Side	Edge	
	Vertex	Vertex
1	1	4
	4	3
	3	2
	2	1
2	2	3
	3	7
	7	6
	6	2
3	6	7
	7	8
	8	5
	5	6
4	5	8
	8	4
	4	1
	1	5
5	7	3
	3	4
	4	8
	8	7
6	6	5
	5	1
	1	2
	2	6

reflections. Well, even though we have added an extra dimension, the same manipulation can be applied; and to keep my explanation consistent, I shall demonstrate the actions using the same image.

Figure 8.3 illustrates a letter 'T' in 3D space with the following coordinates:

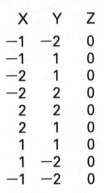

X	Y	Z
−1	−2	0
−1	1	0
−2	1	0
−2	2	0
2	2	0
2	1	0
1	1	0
1	−2	0
−1	−2	0

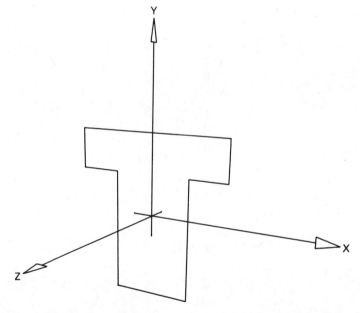

Figure 8.3 Here the letter 'T' is shown in 3D space where every Z-coordinate is zero.

Notice that all the Z-coordinates are zero because the shape exists entirely in the plane where Z equals zero.

Now if a program were to manipulate the coordinates by adding 1 to every X-coordinate the following coordinates result, which are illustrated in Figure 8.4.

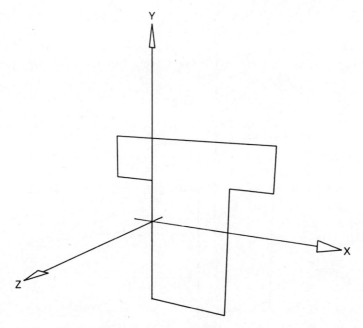

Figure 8.4 The original shape shown in Figure 8.3 has been displaced one unit in the X-direction by adding 1 to the X-coordinates.

X	Y	Z
0	−2	0
0	1	0
−1	1	0
−1	2	0
3	2	0
3	1	0
2	1	0
2	−2	0
0	−2	0

Notice that the image—like the 2D case—causes a shift along the X-axis and, obviously, if the Y-coordinates had been manipulated the shift would have been vertical. The Z-axis has no special properties and behaves in exactly the same way as the X and Y. So one would expect the shape to move forward if the Z-coordinates were increased. In fact it does, and Figure 8.5 shows the effect of increasing all the Z-coordinates by 1.

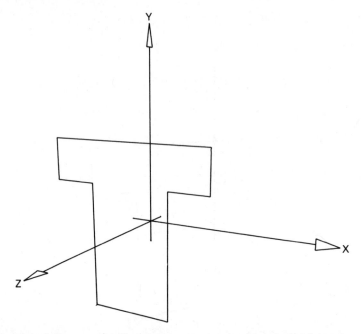

Figure 8.5 The letter 'T' moves along the Z-axis by incrementing the Z-coordinates.

So we see that the effects of two-dimensional shifting still hold in three dimensions, which is not too surprising, and we would not be considered mathematically presumptious if we presumed that multiplying 3D coordinates produced a similar size change. It is left to the inquisitive reader to confirm these results.

8.3 3D reflections

Reflections in two-dimensional space were relative to a line, whereas in three-dimensional space they are relative to a plane. To illustrate this idea, consider the arrangement of an object and mirror plane shown in Figure 8.6. The object is situated such that all of its Z-coordinates are positive, and the reflecting plane contains the X and Y-axes. The reflection can be created simply by reversing the Z-coordinates of the object, which was the technique employed in the two-dimensional case.

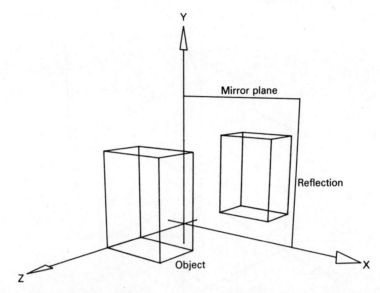

Figure 8.6 Simple reflections can be achieved by the sign reversal of coordinates, in this example the Z-coordinates have been reversed.

Obviously, a reflecting plane can be placed anywhere in space, and at any angle, but an object's reflection cannot be computed simply by reversing one or two coordinates. Under these conditions one must resort to mathematics to resolve the problem, which demands an understanding of trigonometry and geometry. The essential point to understand here is that these formulae can be incorporated within a computer program, which can then undertake the coordinate manipulation.

8.4 3D rotations

In two dimensions one considers a rotation about a point, whereas in three, rotations are about a line or an axis. Figure 8.7 shows a box located at the origin, and a view of it rotated about the vertical Y-axis. Inspection of this image will confirm that the Y-coordinates of the object are unchanged, whereas the X and Z-coordinates are modified. In fact, they are modified by the formulae used in rotating X and Y-coordinates in

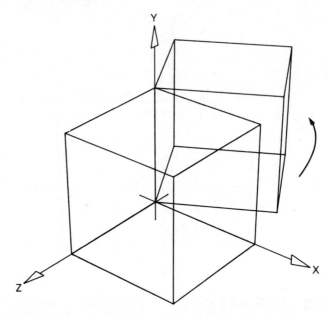

Figure 8.7 Rotating this box about the Y-axis has only altered the X and Z-coordinates.

the two-dimensional case. Furthermore, one could conclude that rotating about the X-axis leaves the X-coordinates unchanged and about the Z-axis, the Z-coordinates remain constant. Anyone skilled in this type of geometry can easily construct the logic necessary to rotate any object about one of the three spatial axes.

Another useful program would be the ability to rotate an object any angle about any axis orientated in space as shown in Figure 8.8. Naturally this is possible, but the mathematics is beyond the scope of this book.

So now we have seen how objects are defined, shifted, scaled, reflected and rotated, but the most important action to consider is how a perspective view is obtained.

8.5 Perspective views of 3D objects

In the previous section we discovered that objects are defined as a collection of facets, made up of edges each consisting of two vertices, defined by three coordinates. Now we need a

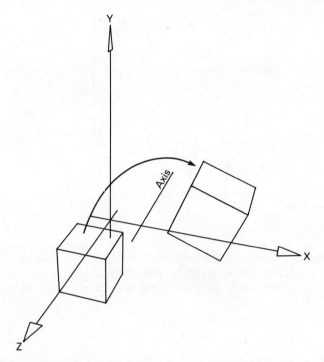

Figure 8.8 A useful facility is to rotate an object about any 3D axis.

mechanism to create a perspective view and fortunately this is not too difficult.

To begin with I shall propose that certain pre-conditions exist to enable me to explain the idea, and later I will develop the explanation such that it is free of any constraints. The conditions are:

- that the computer's eye is located at the origin, and looks along the Z-axis;
- that the object is located somewhere along the Z-axis, and a possible scene is shown in Figure 8.9.

Now in Figure 8.10 the scene has been extended by including a picture plane, with lines connecting the eye to every vertex of the object. Notice that every point in 3D space is transformed into a point upon the picture plane relative to a 2D set of axes and produces a view as shown in Figure 8.11.

The mathematics of this computation is trivial and is

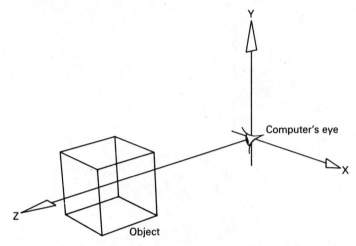

Figure 8.9 To simplify the explanation of perspective drawing, the computer's 'eye' is positioned at the origin looking along the Z-axis, with the object within its field of view.

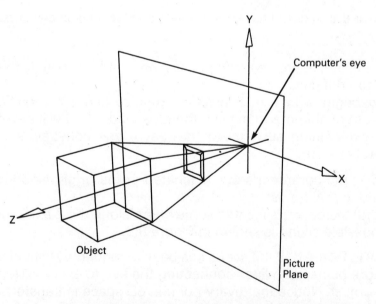

Figure 8.10 A picture plane is used to intersect lines joining the computer's 'eye' to the object. The points of intersection are used to construct the perspective view.

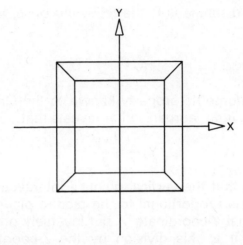

Figure 8.11 A view of a cube as seen by the computer's 'eye'.

explained as follows. Consider Figure 8.12, which shows a side view of the above experiment though for purposes of clarity I have only included one point of the object. What we need to find is the vertical point of intersection on the picture plane represented by Y_2 in the diagram.

Given that the coordinates of the point are (x, y, z) and the

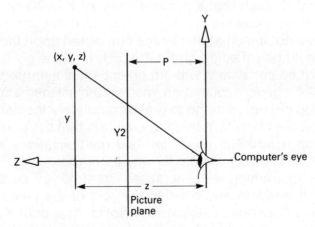

Figure 8.12 This illustrates the geometry employed to compute the value of Y2.

picture plane distance is P, the following observation can be made:

$$\frac{Y_2}{P} = \frac{y}{z}$$

(which is a geometric property known to the Greeks!) So to compute Y_2, a little reorganisation reveals that:

$$Y_2 = \frac{P \cdot y}{z}$$

which means that the vertical point of intersection upon the picture plane is proportional to the picture plane distance P, and the original Y-coordinate y, but inversely proportional to the Z value. It is this division by the Z-coordinate which provides the perspective, i.e. things at a distance appear smaller.

Similarly it can be shown that

$$X_2 = \frac{-P \cdot x}{z}$$

Now what does all this mean? It means that any point in space (x, y, z) can be transformed into another point (X_2, Y_2) as shown in Figure 8.13; and these points when connected correctly will form a perspective image upon the picture plane. The negative sign in the X_2 calculation is included to reverse the sign of X_2 such that a positive value of X in 3D space also has a positive value when transformed upon the picture plane. If this were not included, the image computed upon the picture plane would be reflected about the picture plane's Y-axis, and would not be consistent with an object's real symmetry.

Now the above explanation was rather mathematical, and even if you did not manage to grasp completely the underlying geometry, the important thing to realise is that the perspective calculation is nothing more than two multiplications and two divisions—extremely simple for any computer.

Before examining a generalised method of perspective viewing, it is worth appreciating the role of the picture plane distance in the above calculations. Notice that both X_2 and Y_2 are directly proportional to P, which means that as P is increased in value, so X_2 and Y_2 increase proportionally. Well,

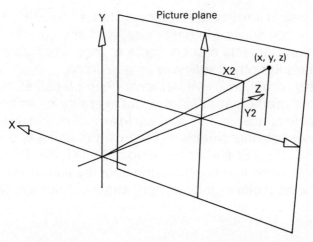

Figure 8.13 Any point (x, y, z) can be transformed into another point (X2, Y2) upon a picture plane, by tracing a line back to the eye and noting the intersection with the picture plane.

we have already seen that size changes are produced by multiplying coordinates, which implies that changing P alters the image size, thus it should be seen as a 'zoom' control for the computer's eye.

The degree of perspective is determined by the eye's distance from the object and totally independent of P. Figure 8.14 shows two views of the same object; one drawn close with a small picture plane distance, and the other drawn at a

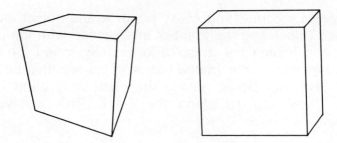

Figure 8.14 Here we see two views of the same coordinates; the left, close up with a small picture plane distance, and the right, a distant view with a large picture plane distance.

distance with a large picture plane distance. Thus it is possible to achieve any sense of spatial size from any coordinates; on the one hand objects can be made to look small as a match-box, and on the other, massive as a building.

Now the computer's eye has only been placed at the origin to keep the mathematics simple, but in reality it can be placed anywhere in space, and be looking in any direction. Figure 8.15 illustrates a possible situation. The position of the eye is speci-fied by (XE, YE, ZE) and its focal point by (XF, YF, ZF); the line connecting these two points represents the line of sight which intersects the picture plane at right angles. A perspective view

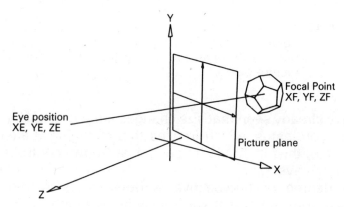

Figure 8.15 It must be possible to locate the eye position and focal point anywhere in space.

is formed by connecting every point on the object with the eye, and calculating the point of intersection with the picture plane, and joining the dots. Unfortunately, when the eye is floating in space, the mathematics of perspective becomes rather nasty, but can be greatly simplified by locating the eye at the origin looking along the Z-axis. This involves the following:

● subtract XE, YE, ZE from the object's coordinates;
● rotate them such that the line of sight is coincident with the Z-axis; again this is a trivial exercise for a computer pro-grammer.

So whenever a perspective view is required of an object, the following information is required:

- the position of the eye
- the position of the focal point
- the picture plane distance
- the coordinates representing the object.

During the execution of a computer program the coordinates undergo two transformations. Originally, they are specified in world coordinates, they are then translated into eye coordinates—which is when the eye is positioned at the origin—and, finally, are transformed into screen coordinates, which are displayed upon a graph plotter or graphic screen.

In the author's computer graphic system PICASO, the location of the computer's eye is specified by the command:

CALL EYE (XE, YE, ZE, XF, YF, ZF)

where (XE, YE, ZE) locates the position of the eye relative to the origin, and (XF, YF, ZF) identifies the focal point. If a 3D drawing command is given, the computer creates a perspective view of an object as seen from that position. The following program statements instruct the computer to input a file of 3D coordinates and display them from a given location.

CALL IN3D(OBJECT, 'AHOUSE')
CALL EYE(15.0, 15.0, 15.0, 0.0, 0.0, 0.0)
CALL DRAWIT(OBJECT)

The 'IN3D' command inputs a file of 3D coordinates called 'AHOUSE' from the computer's disks, and loads them into memory under the name 'OBJECT'. The 'EYE' command places the observer at X=15.0, Y=15.0, Z=15.0 looking towards the origin. Finally, the 'DRAWIT' command displays the perspective view from this position.

Perhaps now it can be seen how powerful the computer becomes as a visualisation tool for viewing 3D scenes. So long as it is possible to supply a collection of 3D coodinates, the computer can produce any perspective view simply by providing six numbers: three for the eye position and three for the focal point. Indeed, I am sure some readers have already anticipated how the computer can be used to generate an animated sequence of images, but before explaining this in detail, it is necessary to investigate procedures for removing certain lines that should not be seen.

8.6 Hidden-line removal

The formulae developed in the previous section were totally insensitive to whether certain coordinates of an object could be seen or not. Consequently they produce images similar to that shown in Figure 8.16, where every edge is seen: which is

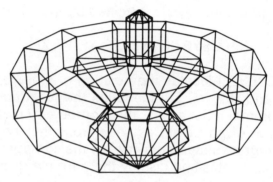

Figure 8.16 This confusing wire frame image is due to the fact that perspective calculations do not test for the visibility of an edge.

why they are referred to as wire frame images. Under some circumstances this is not a problem, but when objects are constructed from hundreds, or even thousands, of edges it is virtually impossible to discern their basic structural properties.

In the evolution of computer graphics, considerable effort has been devoted to the problem of hidden-line removal, resulting in a whole variety of programming techniques to resolve the problem. The fine logical detail of these algorithms (procedures) is totally beyond the scope of this book, but it is possible to examine some of the strategies employed to appreciate the magnitude of the problem.

If only the computer could 'see' what it was doing, the problem of hidden-line removal would not arise, but as the machine is 'blind' it is necessary to formulate a sequence of tests that can be applied so that certain lines can be rejected on geometric grounds, and on our own experience of three-dimensional space.

One very simple test on the visibility of a surface is based upon observations associated with objects known as convex objects—e.g. boxes, cones, cylinders and pyramids. For when one looks at any convex object, one side can never mask another, which implies that any side is either completely visible or completely invisible. In the case of a box, a typical view would only reveal three sides, with the remaining three sides invisible.

If it were possible to devise a way of identifying the invisible sides from the visible, the problem of individual convex objects would be solved. There is a solution and its mechanism is extremely simple. It relies upon the assumption that only one side of a facet can ever be visible, so that when an object is created numerically, the mathematical techniques describing the facets clearly identify the facet's visible side. This is achieved by associating a line with each facet called a normal vector, which is at right-angles (normal) to the surface, pointing away from its visible side. Figure 8.17 illustrates two facets, one seen by the computer's eye, and the other invisible. Notice that when a line is connected from the eye to the base of these normal vectors, the enclosed angle can be used to determine visibility. For if the angle is between 0° and 90° the facet is visible, but if it exceeds 90° it is invisible.

Again, the mathematics describing this geometry is relatively simple and can be easily incorporated within computer programs. Figure 8.18 shows a variety of convex objects that have been drawn with back faces removed. This removal is known as culling.

Unfortunately, back face removal does not resolve the masking of one object by another, or objects containing holes or concavities, but it does provide an efficient method for simplifying the data. To achieve total hidden-line removal every edge must be examined for interference with other edges, which can be a time-consuming operation requiring programs that

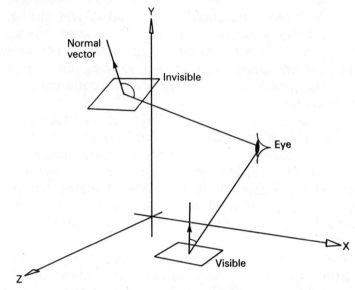

Figure 8.17 To assist in the detection of surface visibility, each facet has associated with it a line called a normal vector. If the angle between this vector and another connecting it to the eye exceeds 90°, the surface is invisible.

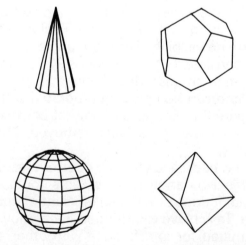

Figure 8.18 Four convex objects drawn with back faces removed.

have anticipated every possible orientation of two edges. Figure 8.19 illustrates the application of hidden-line removal upon a complex industrial object.

Hidden-line removal programs must not only resolve the view as 'seen' by the computer, but also ensure that co-ordinates behind the observer, or out of the field of vision, are not displayed. The removal of this detail is called 'clipping' and is performed before hidden-line removal algorithms are applied. Clipping also needs mathematical procedures to assist in these tests, but can be described as follows.

Consider the scene illustrated in Figure 8.20, where an observer is looking towards an object. If the picture plane is marked with four points representing the limiting viewing area, they can be joined to the observer to form a pyramid

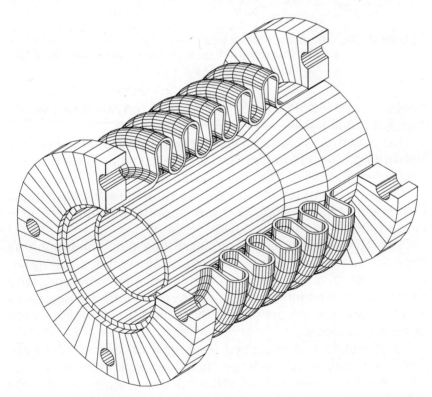

Figure 8.19 Hidden-line removal applied to an object created using a CAD system.

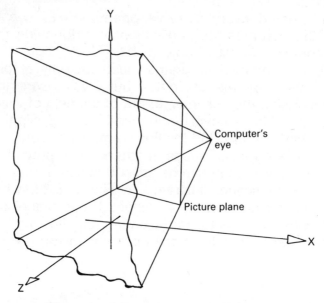

Figure 8.20 The computer's 'eye' only sees what is contained
within the pyramid formed by joining lines from the
picture plane limits to the eye.

containing all visible elements. Anything not contained within
this volume is not seen.

This volume is constrained further by two other planes
preventing objects too near and too far from being seen, these
are generally called the 'near' and 'far' planes. Figure 8.21
reveals the completed viewing frustum. Once coordinates
have been clipped against these boundaries, they are processed for hidden-line removal.

Clipping programs are essential in computer animation as
the computer's 'eye' is moved dynamically within a configura-
tion of coordinates, some in front and others behind; and
unless these unseen data are removed, computer programs
would draw out objects physically behind them, which would
appear ridiculous.

So to obtain a perspective view of a collection of 3D coordinates they must undergo three separate manipulations:
first, the original world coordinates are translated into eye
coordinates; second, they are clipped; and third, they are processed for hidden-line removal.

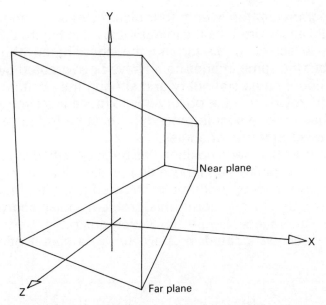

Figure 8.21 Before hidden-line removal is attempted, edges are clipped against the six planes comprising the viewing frustum.

8.7 3D image manipulation

Three-dimensional programming is no more complicated than working in two dimensions, for so long as the position of the observer is known, the perspective transformation is undertaken by the computer and is totally transparent to the user. To illustrate this point, the following program demonstrates how a computer program can create a sequence of images showing an object spinning in space. The program stages are:

Example 1

(a) Input a collection of 3D coordinates.
(b) Define the position of an observer.
(c) Repeat stages (e) to (f) twenty-four times.
(d) Stop.
(e) Display a perspective view of the coordinates.
(f) Rotate the coordinates 15° around the vertical y-axis.

This program creates twenty-four pictures of a rotating object and could easily produce the images shown in Figure 8.22. The rotation is achieved by turning the coordinates about the Y-axis, but the same images could have been created by keeping the coordinates stationary and altering the position of the observer. However, if the observer is to move in a circular path about the Y-axis, a simple procedure must be found to locate the observer in terms of angles.

So far, the observer's position has been specified in terms of Cartesian coordinates and these do not allow it to be moved in angular movements, without a knowledge of trigonometry and geometry. To overcome this problem, polar coordinates can be employed. Figure 8.23 demonstrates how a 3D observer can be located in space using angles. Notice that

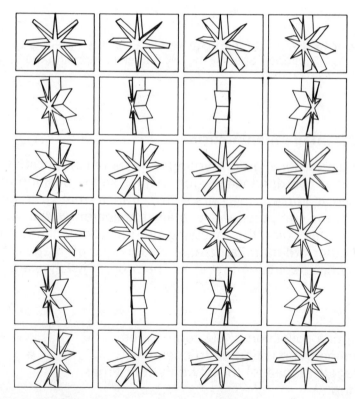

Figure 8.22 These pictures were created by rotating the 3D co-ordinates of the star about the vertical Y-axis.

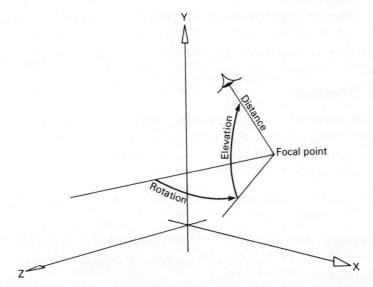

Figure 8.23 Defining the observer in polar coordinates facilitates the control of angular movements.

once a focal point has been identified, the observer is placed a specified distance away looking back along the Z-direction. Then an angle of rotation sweeps it horizontally around this point, and an angle of elevation vertically above the ground plane. The user still has to supply six numbers: three for the focal point, one for the distance and two angles, rotation and elevation. But this method of locating the observer is frequently more effective than a Cartesian definition. Though it might be more convenient for a user, the observer's position must ultimately be specified in Cartesian form, but this can be calculated by the computer.

If the above program was specified in polar coordinates it would become:

(a) Input a collection of 3D coordinates.
(b) Define the position of an observer in polar form: distance, rotation and elevation.
(c) Repeat stages (e) to (f) twenty-four times.
(d) Stop.
(e) Display a perspective view of the coordinates.
(f) Change the eye's angle of rotation by 15°.

This program creates the same graphic output as the previous one, but is much more flexible for purposes of animation; but more of this in Chapter 10, section 2.

8.8 Summary

In this section I have deliberately avoided the procedures for constructing objects, and concentrated upon simple methods for processing coordinates and obtaining perspective views. The salient points to remember are:

- Cartesian coordinates can be used to define the structure of a 3D object.

- Objects are generally constructed from a hierarchical description of facets, composed of edges, which in turn have two vertices.

- 3D coordinates—like 2D coordinates—can be manipulated arithmetically resulting in shifting, scaling, reflecting and rotating.

- A collection of 3D coordinates can be transformed into a two-dimensional perspective view by introducing the location of an observer and the idea of a picture plane.

- Because the computer is conceptually 'blind', detail which normally would be invisible to a human eye is removed by hidden-line procedures.

- The process of clipping removes detail physically behind the observer or out of view.

- The observer's position must ultimately be in Cartesian form but is often expressed in polar coordinates to facilitate angular movements.

9 3D modelling

'Castles in the air—they're so easy to take refuge in. So easy to build too.'

Henrik Ibsen

Three-dimensional modelling is an extremely important aspect of computer graphics and indeed Computer Aided Design Systems. It has been researched into over several years, and there are new ideas and techniques continuously being discovered to ease the modelling of different objects. For example, just consider the problems of modelling the following objects: boxes, spheres, vases, cups, boats, planes, hands, heads, skeletons, buildings, water, clouds, fire, grass, etc. A tremendous variety of subjects each exhibiting special surface properties requires different solutions to represent their forms in a computer system. I will now approach the problems of modelling starting with simple files of coordinates and finishing with fractal surfaces, which can be used to represent mountain ranges.

9.1 Coordinate files

In Chapter 8 I illustrated how Cartesian coordinates could be used to define vertices, which could form edges, which in turn formed facets. From these facets a solid object could be modelled. This basic modelling technique is fundamental to computer graphics and should be understood completely, especially if the reader is to grasp the concepts of shading and illumination.

Just imagine that it is necessary to model numerically the object shown in Figure 9.1. Each vertex has been labelled with its coordinates, and one notices that the object is constructed from five surfaces, each expressed in terms of these vertices. Table 9.1 defines each surface in turn.

These coordinates could easily be constructed as a computer file and stored upon a disk storage system. Once the data has

Table 9.1

	X	Y	Z
Surface 1	0	0	1
	0	1	1
	1	1	0
	1	0	0
	0	0	1
Surface 2	0	1	1
	0	2	0
	1	1	0
	0	1	1
Surface 3	1	0	0
	1	1	0
	0	2	0
	0	0	0
	1	0	0
Surface 4	0	0	0
	0	2	0
	0	1	1
	0	0	1
	0	0	0
Surface 5	0	0	1
	1	0	0
	0	0	0
	0	0	1

been stored, a program can be instructed to retrieve it and produce a perspective view from a specified eye position. This method of modelling is very simple and would only be employed with objects constructed from a few sides.

To avoid the repetition of a vertex two or three times, it is possible to number the vertices and then define the facets in

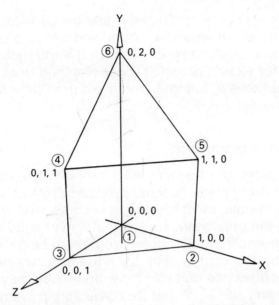

Figure 9.1 This simple object can be modelled by constructing it from a collection of planar facets, composed of vertex sequences.

terms of these numbers. For example, if the above vertices were numbered:

vertex number	X	Y	Z
1	0	0	0
2	1	0	0
3	0	0	1
4	0	1	1
5	1	1	0
6	0	2	0

The surfaces would be:

surface 1   3, 4, 5, 2, 3
surface 2   4, 6, 5, 4
surface 3   2, 5, 6, 1, 2
surface 4   1, 6, 4, 3, 1
surface 5   3, 2, 1, 3

The advantage of this technique is that the surfaces have been defined in terms of vertex numbers, and just by altering the X, Y, Z values of one vertex, it is reflected throughout the entire model. If, for example, vertex 6 was changed from (0, 2, ,0) to (0, 3, 0) surfaces 2, 3 and 4 would automatically register this alteration.

9.2 Graphic primitives

Certain objects can be built into computer graphic systems such as: cubes, boxes, cones, cylinders, pyramids, etc. The cube, for example, must have eight vertices, twelve edges and six sides—the only characteristic that can change is the edge length. This enables a computer program to be designed without knowing the edge length, for if the program has stored a cube with edges one unit long, any other cube may be formed by multiplying the X, Y and Z-coordinates by some suitable scaling factor.

Similarly, boxes, cones and other regular objects may be stored as a unit size and scaled by the user. The storing of these graphic primitives permits the construction of more complex objects from these basic building elements. Figure 9.2 demonstrates how a model can be constructed entirely from boxes.

9.3 Thin models

Say it was required to obtain some perspective views of a two-dimensional image. This could be achieved very quickly by first digitizing the image and storing it upon a disk file. A program could then input these coordinates and process them such that a Z-coordinate of zero was associated with each vertex. This effectively creates a wafer-thin object standing in the X–Y plane as shown in Figure 9.3.

By establishing a 3D observer within the computer program, it is possible to display any perspective view of the original image. Figure 9.4 shows three perspective views of a 2D map of the world—notice that if the eye had been looking directly along the X or Y-axis, the resulting drawing would have been a line.

Figure 9.2 These tables and chairs are constructed from simple blocks.

9.4 Extruded models

A natural development of thin objects is to model thick objects, i.e. objects having depth, but with constant cross-section. Figure 9.5 illustrates this idea applied to the letter 'H'. Here we see that the 3D model has been formed by extruding the original 2D shape in the Z-direction.

Extruding is a simple geometric process and does not require any sophisticated programming. The model shown in Figure 9.5 is formed from a front and back view of the letter 'H' with twelve rectangular facets forming the extruded surface. Thus every edge on the original 2D shape will generate a facet joining front to back.

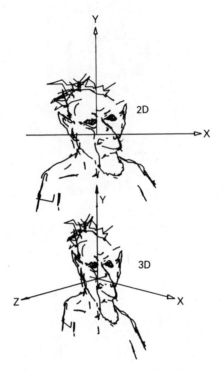

Figure 9.3 Wafer-thin models may be formed from 2D images and associating a Z-coordinate of zero with each vertex.

Figure 9.6 shows how useful this extruding technique could be in computer-based graphic design systems, whereby the system could supply many views of an extruded shape with different depths.

9.5 Swept surfaces

Swept surfaces, or surfaces of revolution, provide a powerful modelling technique for creating really complex objects. The one constraint imposed upon the modeller is that the required model must have rotational symmetry about one axis. This simply means that it must be possible to create the surface by sweeping a contour, or contours, about some axis.

To create a wine glass, as an example, all that is required is one contour which can be swept about the vertical Y-axis.

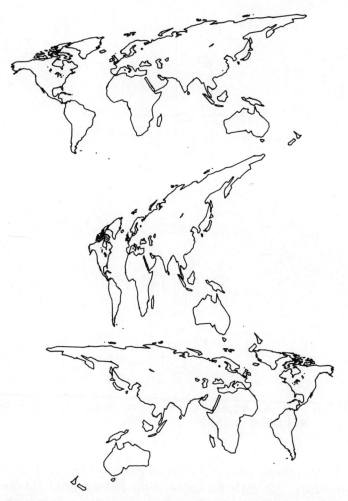

Figure 9.4 Three perspective views of a 2D map of the world.

Figure 9.7 shows a single contour which when rotated in twenty steps, forms a faceted model of a glass. The final model has no thickness, but could have had, if the original contour contained this information.

One obvious feature of this technique, is the ability to generate a family of related objects by varying the number of rotational steps in the final surface. Figure 9.8 shows three views of models formed with different rotational steps.

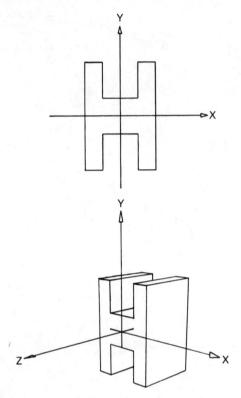

Figure 9.5 The 2D letter 'H' has been used to create the 3D extruded model.

The final model is stored as a collection of facets which are generated by the vertices making up the original 2D contour. This implies that if there are n vertices on the original contour, there must be $n-1$ edges for constructing facets. Also, if there are m rotational steps the final model will contain:

$$m\ (n-1)\ \text{facets.}$$

So this can lead to some numerically large coordinate files if both n and m are large.

Swept surfaces can also be used for modelling spherical surfaces. In fact a sphere is formed by sweeping a semi-circle through 360°. Figure 9.9 illustrates the modelling of a sphere and two other models containing curved surfaces.

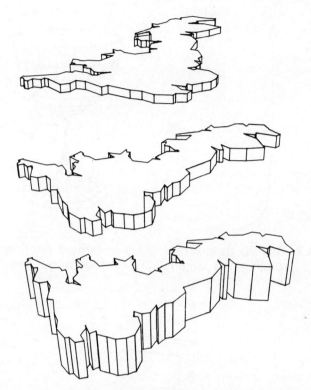

Figure 9.6 These three views of Great Britain demonstrate the effect of altering the depth of extrusion.

In all the examples so far, the swept contour has been cut by the Y-axis. If now the contour is closed and moved away from the Y-axis, doughnut-like objects are formed. To illustrate this, consider the consequences of sweeping an off-centre rectangle in four stages. Figure 9.10 shows the result which is in the form of a picture frame. So to model a doughnut all that is needed is to sweep an off-centre circle through 360° as shown in Figure 9.11.

Finally, Figure 9.12 illustrates a model which has been constructed entirely from swept surfaces, and remember, computer models—no matter how they are created—can always be combined together to form a collective solution to a problem.

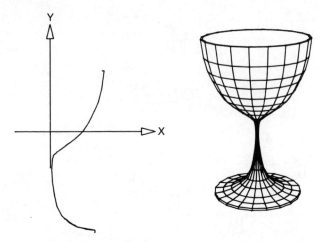

Figure 9.7 This 3D model of a glass is formed geometrically by rotating the original 2D contour about the Y-axis in twenty steps.

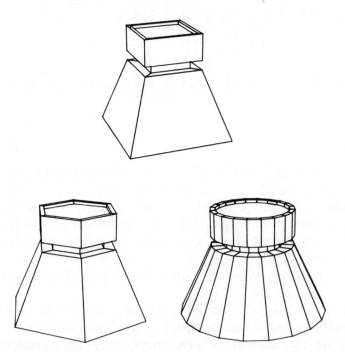

Figure 9.8 Three models created by sweeping a contour with different numbers of steps.

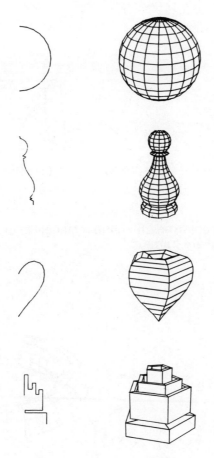

Figure 9.9 Three different models created by swept surfaces.

9.6 Ruled surfaces

Ruled surfaces are used to model structures such as the wing of an aircraft. They are formed by joining together two separate boundary contours with straight lines. Figure 9.13 shows two closed contours displaced along the Z-axis and joined together with straight lines. Unlike the modelling techniques discussed so far, this method can create twisted facets which might upset shading programs and hidden-line removal algorithms.

There are really no rules to say what contours may be used

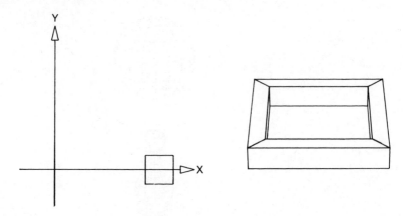

Figure 9.10 Sweeping an off-centre rectangle in four stages creates a square frame.

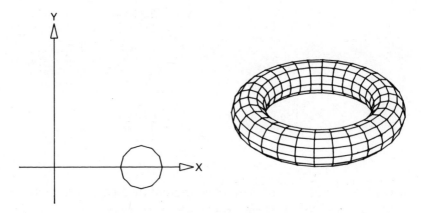

Figure 9.11 A doughnut can be modelled by sweeping an off-centre circle through 360°.

or not. If the user wishes to construct a strange surface, it can generally be achieved, but if the resulting facet is twisted or interpenetrates another, this can cause problems. Figure 9.14 illustrates an unusual application of ruled surfaces.

9.7 Wrapping

The modelling procedures employed in computer graphic systems are greatly influenced by whether the final image is to

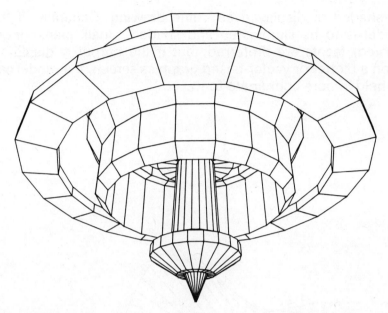

Figure 9.12 This model has been created entirely from swept surfaces.

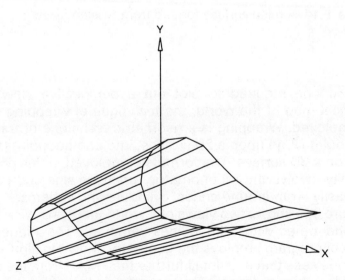

Figure 9.13 This ruled surface is formed by joining two separate contours with lines.

be shaded or displayed as a line drawing. Generally, if the model is to be illuminated and shaded, small, planar (non-twisted) facets are preferred; but if the output is displayed upon a plotter or vector-based graphics screen, the model can be held in pure coordinate form.

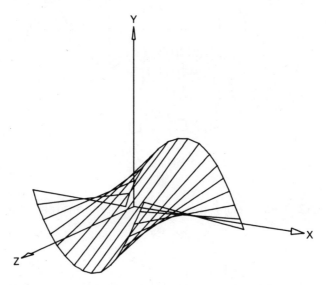

Figure 9.14 A ruled surface formed from twisted facets.

So, if one required to plot out a perspective view of a spherical map of the world, the technique of wrapping could be employed. Wrapping is a geometric technique of translating a point (x, y) upon a 2D surface, into another point (x', y', z') upon a 3D surface. The formulae employed in this process typically involve the trigonometric functions sine and cosine, and easily wrap around cones, cylinders and spheres.

Figure 9.15 shows two views of a world map, one wire-frame and the other with hidden-lines removed. The hidden-line removal program employs the geometry shown in Figure 9.16. Here one sees that any detail further than MAX from the eye is invisible, which means that every vertex is tested for this limiting distance before being displayed.

Figure 9.15 These globes have been created by wrapping a 2D map about a sphere.

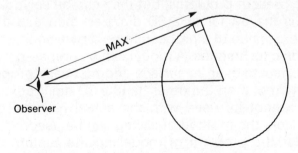

Figure 9.16 The observer cannot see detail on the sphere when it is beyond the limiting distance MAX.

9.8 Parametric techniques

The observant reader should have noticed that I have not resorted to mathematical ideas beyond high-school geometry. However, there are many instances within modelling where very sophisticated mathematical concepts are employed to describe complex three-dimensional surfaces. As an example, just consider the problems of describing in coordinate form the surface description of a teapot, with handle and spout. Perhaps the body of the teapot can be formed by a swept surface, but the handle and spout raise serious questions as to the choice of modelling technique.

Parametric surface description permits this type of modelling, but the mathematical description is totally beyond the scope of this book, and even then, would only interest a programmer implementing these techniques. However, it is worth mentioning that various techniques have been developed to solve the problems of modelling complex surfaces. Some of the most well-known surface descriptions are: linear Coons surfaces (Coons, S.A.), Bicubic Surface Patches, Bézier Surfaces (Bézier, P.E.) and B-Spline Surfaces. They all exhibit certain weaknesses and strengths and are employed in industrial CAD systems to cope with surfaces found in aircraft, cars, propellers and machine tools.

9.9 Manual methods

So far we have discovered how to model regular objects such as: cones, cylinders, glasses, aircraft wings and teapots. But what about asymmetric objects like: hands, heads and feet? These do present problems, but they can be solved.

If one is the owner of a 3D digitizer, then this device can locate the position of a probe in three dimensions, using sonic or electronic techniques. A model can be prepared by drawing triangular facets over its surface and manually probing it one facet at a time. If on the other hand a 3D digitizer is not available, or cannot be used with the actual physical model for some reason, the method of slicing can be used.

Consider the problem of modelling the Statute of Liberty with the eventual objective of displaying it in colour. This can be achieved by the following steps:

(a) Make a model in plaster about 18" high.
(b) Place the model in a rigid rectangular container and fill the vacant space with a coloured form of plaster or resin.
(c) Cut the complete structure into thin slices—say about 0.25" each.
(d) Digitize each sliced contour with the same number of vertices, using a corner as an origin.
(e) Load the digitized contours into a computer program to construct a triangulated surface.

Figure 9.17 shows a final view of the model, but notice that not all the elements were modelled in this way; others have been added by other techniques, because the slicing approach limits the degree of detail detected. A final shaded view of the statue is shown in Plate 2.

9.10 Fractals

Fractal geometry is concerned with describing curves and surfaces that appear random, but in fact exhibit properties of self-similarity. Before considering the three-dimensional type, it will be useful to consider and understand the simpler two-dimensional version.

Consider the situation in Figure 9.18 where it is necessary to connect points A and B together with a pseudo-random line. This can be achieved by dividing the line in two, to create a centre point C. A further point D, can be identified which is some random distance at right-angles to C. Now we have two line segments: AD and DB, and if the same fractal division process is continued on these segments, a fractal curve results. Figure 9.19 shows a fractal curve created in this way.

One important feature of this technique, is that the co-ordinates of the fractal have not necessarily to be stored. For so long as the end points are available, and the pseudo-random number generator program, it can be created by re-calculating the coordinates. Now in three dimensions, this last property is very important, because fractal surfaces could require very large numbers of coordinates.

A similar idea of division is also applied in fractal surfaces as shown in Figure 9.20. Here we see a facet ABCD which has

Figure 9.17 This is a triangulated model created by digitizing a statue in slices.

been divided into four smaller random facets. This can be achieved in a variety of ways. Initially the four edges are randomly divided to produce the points H, I, J, K and F. From these points the new facets AHFK, HBIF, ICJF, JDKF are formed. This subdivision process can be continued until suffi-

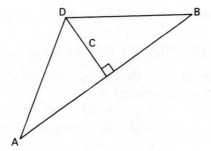

Figure 9.18 This illustrates the first stage of a fractal curve, whereby the point D has been used to divide the original line segment in two.

Figure 9.19 This fractal curve has been created by continually sub-dividing line segments into smaller segments.

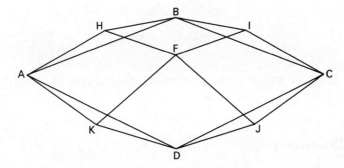

Figure 9.20 The facet ABCD can be divided into four smaller facets, by choosing the points H, I, J, and K such that they subdivide the original edges with a random displacement. F is also computed along these lines.

cient detail has been achieved. Figure 9.21 illustrates a fractal created using a similar division process.

The two important properties of fractals are that:

- they can be regenerated by a program and therefore do not have to be held in coordinate form;
- the subdivision process can always be continued until the smallest facet is beyond the resolution of the display system.

Fractals have been employed in various animation sequences which demonstrate the ability to fly over imaginary landscapes, without actually having to model the terrain.

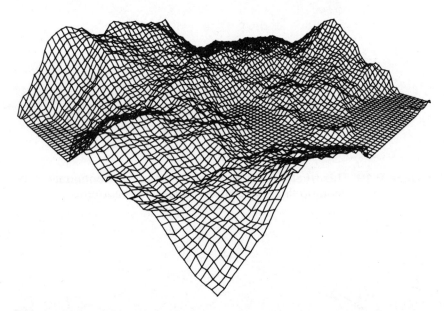

Figure 9.21 A fractal surface formed by a process of subdivision.

9.11 Summary

As we have seen, modelling consists of a wide variety of techniques employed to generate coordinates, which can be manipulated by computer programs. Here, then are some important points to remember:

- Simple models can be analysed visually, and coordinate files formed from the individual facet descriptions.

- One convenient data structure is to number each vertex and describe each facet in terms of these vertex numbers.

- Many CAD modelling systems employ the idea of graphic primitives from which complex models may be formed.

- Thin three-dimensional surfaces can be created from two-dimensional images by giving each vertex a Z value of zero.

- Thick three-dimensional models are easily formed by extruding two-dimensional contours.

- Swept surfaces or surfaces of revolution create models that have a rotational symmetry about an axis.

- Ruled surfaces are formed by joining together two contours with straight lines.

- Wrapping is a geometric technique of transforming two-dimensional coordinates into three-dimensional surfaces such as cones, cylinders and spheres.

- Parametric curves are mathematical models for describing complex smooth surfaces.

- Manual methods of slicing are often necessary to model highly irregular objects.

- Fractals are useful in describing semi-random structures such as mountain ranges.

10   3D monochrome applications

'Architecture in general is frozen music.'
Friedrich von Schelling

Chapters 8 and 9 revealed the programming principles behind 3D computer graphic systems, and the techniques of 3D modelling. This insight stands us in good stead to investigate some of the applications for these ideas. I have chosen three separate subject areas which are becoming increasingly influenced by computer graphic systems, namely: technical illustration, animation and architecture.

10.1   Technical illustration

The illustration of engineering machinery is bound to become computerised as CAD systems are absorbed into the original design activity. Already, in the automotive, ship and aviation-based industries, computer graphic systems are depended upon to maintain the complex drawings required for design work. These working drawings will ultimately become available for any illustrative activity associated with the component. Thus future technical illustrators will be able to rely upon powerful computer design systems, supplying perspective views of any complex assembly, with partial cross-sections, explosions and component identification.

These systems are already being exploited in technical support documentation which generally require hundreds of detailed accurate drawings to illustrate technical, servicing and training manuals. As an example, Figure 10.1 illustrates a cut-away view of a heat-exchanger generated by a modern CAD system. Once the model has been created within a computer system, it is extremely easy to generate any view of this assembly, saving a technical illustrator many man-hours of skilled drafting.

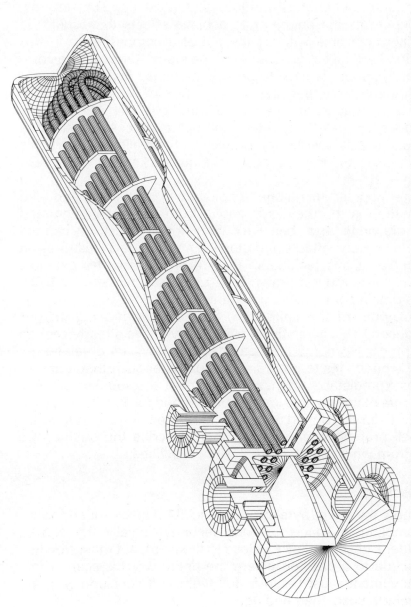

Figure 10.1 This technical illustration has been created by a CAD system which allows it to be viewed from any position in space.

10.2 Animation

Computer animation is undoubtedly an exciting subject area, as it permits the animator to achieve effects that would be totally impossible without the aid of a computer. So in this section I will investigate some of the ways monochrome computer systems are used to provide animated images.

Although computer graphic systems can generate amazing coloured images, monochrome output is still considerably cheaper, as relatively little computer processing time is needed to produce the line-drawings. It also allows the graphic designer to explore various techniques to enhance the final images.

One popular technique employed in television and film animation is to create a negative from computer generated line drawings, and then back light under a rostrum camera providing neon effects and glowing lines. Plate 3 illustrates an example of this technique. Plate 4 shows another example where the computer-drawn cells were back-painted and back-lit to obtain some exciting lighting effects.

But what of the animation, how are the moving images produced? This is relatively easy, for we have already seen in Chapter 8, Section 5 how perspective views are obtained. All that is needed is to program the computer such that it undertakes a predictable animated movement and supplies pictures at a rate of twenty-five images per second for British television or thirty for the United States. To illustrate this in greater detail, I shall propose a project and then describe the outline of a program which creates the desired drawings.

Project requirements

Show the word 'byte' modelled in 3D in an extruded form tumbling in space for four seconds. Initially the computer's observer is very close to the word, but must slowly recede to a position where the entire word is seen. The movement must begin in full flight and conclude with a smooth cushioned ending.

The solution to this problem requires a piece of artwork with a flat view of the word 'byte' as shown in Figure 10.2. This can be input to a computer program which can then model a 3D extruded form.

The program outline is as follows:

(a) Input the digitised coordinates for the word 'byte'.
(b) Create a 3D extruded model with the required depth.
(c) Input the starting and finishing positions of the observer in polar coordinates from a disk file.
(d) Repeat stages (f) to (h) one hundred times (4 × 25 for British television).
(e) Stop the computer.

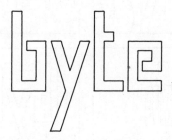

Figure 10.2 This drawing, when digitised, can be used to create an extruded model for animation purposes.

(f) Place the computer's observer at a distance, rotation and elevation dependent upon the current picture number, with cushioning, i.e. as the computer generates pictures, so the observer must move from the starting position to the final position anticipating the end.
(g) Draw a hidden-line view of the word 'byte' from this position.
(h) Select a clean piece of paper.

The above program could be designed to produce the selected images shown in Figure 10.3.

Computer animation sequences can become extremely complex, incorporating all the possible effects such as: transformations, explosions, turning, dynamic observer, varying extrusion depths, etc. See Chapter 13, Section 2 for further examination of animation techniques.

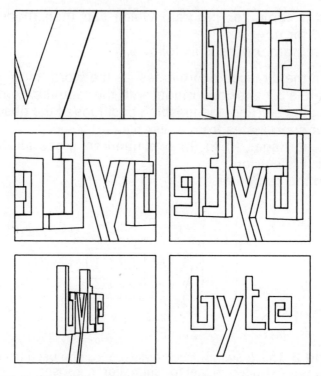

Figure 10.3 These images have been produced by an animation program which has moved the computer's 'eye' through a controlled movement.

10.3 Architecture

Architectural work involves the production and maintenance of 2D and 3D working drawings, and consequently is a natural application for computer graphics. In fact, there are several systems which undertake this type of work, and provide architects with a total package.

A typical system provides facilities including:

- a user-extensible symbol library for components such as: doors, windows, cavity walls, basins, etc.
- the ability to locate services upon different system layers, i.e. wiring diagrams, plumbing routes, gas piping, ventilation ducting, drainage, etc.

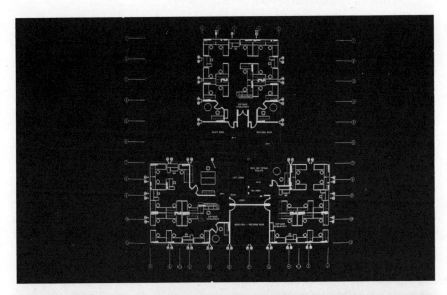

Figure 10.4 Two examples of computer-generated images by an architectural system. (Courtesy: Applied Research of Cambridge Ltd.)

- the stressing of floors, beams and columns for loading levels to meet safety regulations
- the dimensioning of drawings
- the assembly of 2D schematic layouts
- elevations and sectional drawings
- a schedule of components
- costings
- resource planning
- critical path analysis for construction projects
- 3D perspective viewing
- surface rendering
- illumination calculations
- heat loss calculations.

In these situations the computer really excels as a time-saving design tool, and one wonders how architects ever managed to operate without them. Figure 10.4 illustrates two drawings produced by such an architectural system.

10.4 Summary

Computer-based 3D design systems are becoming increasingly employed within a wide variety of manufacturing industries. This utilisation will ultimately have an impact upon other graphical and design activities within these companies, as it seems sensible to establish a common data base of design data, which can be accessed by any artist or designer. The major points raised in this Chapter are:

- CAD systems are able to create highly complex 3D drawings from any view point in space.

- Animated sequences of images are realised by dynamically moving the computer's observer or mathematically manipulating the numerical 3D models.

- Architectural systems employ the modelling features of modern CAD systems, and also incorporate the animated roving computer observer to obtain views of interiors and exteriors before the building is commenced.

11 Shading and realism

'There is nothing ugly; I never saw an ugly thing in my life: for let the form of an object be what it may,—light, shade, and perspective will always make it beautiful.'

John Constable

Very early computer graphic systems only displayed relatively primitive line drawings. But with the progress of television technology, equipment was developed to permit the display of coloured images direct from the computer. The one device that has really influenced the evolution of colour graphics is the frame store, and this device has already been described previously in section 6.2. In the following sections I will describe how shaded pictures are produced and the techniques employed to improve their realism.

11.1 The physics of illumination

Greek philosophers had pondered over the mechanism of colour vision before proposing various theories to explain the sensations of colour. The third-century thinker Plotinus believed that coloured objects could interact directly with our eyes, and the further the objects receded, the more blurred became the colours. Not very convincing, you might think, but neither is the theory of Democritus, who asserted that an object's colour was due to the arrangement of its atoms. White objects had smooth atoms whilst black objects had rough atoms.

Today, we know that our sense of vision is due to sensitivity to a band of the electromagnetic spectrum called light. When this radiation is emitted by a light source, such as a lamp or the sun, some of it is reflected by objects and detected by our eyes. The lens within our eye focuses this radiation upon the retina, which is stimulated electrically; this in turn passes signals to our brain where the sensation of seeing is experienced.

It is not yet possible to model this complex process of seeing within computers, but it is, however, possible to construct computer-generated images which can convince the eye and brain that they are reasonably life-like. To achieve this a program must be capable of controlling the colour of an object, the texture of its surface, and its ability to transmit and refract light.

An object's colour is not an absolute property of the object. It has been shown with many experiments, that because the brain is the source of colour sensation, it can be tricked into creating coloured images that are totally inconsistent. But apart from these anomalies, one can describe the mechanism of surface colour as being caused by an object absorbing certain wavelengths of light and reflecting others. Thus, for example, when a tomato is illuminated with white light, its skin absorbs most of the wavelengths apart from those around 700nm, which causes a red sensation.

As described earlier, the retina's construction enables a wide spectrum of colours to be created from varying amounts of red, green and blue light. This enables a light source within a computer program to be specified in terms of various amounts of red, green and blue light.

Say, for example, it was required to establish a medium-bright yellow light source within a program. This could be represented by 100 units of red, 100 units of green and 50 units of blue, i.e. pale yellow. But what of the object, what is its colour? This could be defined in terms of its ability to reflect red, green and blue light. So we require three coefficients of colour reflection for the object.

If the object were bright blue when illuminated with white light, it implies that the coefficients of reflection are: red = 0.0, green = 0.0 and blue = 1.0. So when it is illuminated with yellow light, the reflected light is computed by multiplying the incident light by the coefficients of reflection, that is:

$$\begin{aligned}
\text{reflected red} &= 100 \times 0.0 = 0.0 \\
\text{reflected green} &= 100 \times 0.0 = 0.0 \\
\text{reflected blue} &= 50 \times 1.0 = 50.0
\end{aligned}$$

Thus the blue object will always appear bluish whilst there is a component of blue in the incident light.

Another property of light radiation is that the further the light source is from an object, the greater the attenuation in intensity. In fact, the final intensity is inversely proportional to the square of the distance between the object and light source. Some computer graphic systems take into account this phenomenon, whilst others ignore it on the grounds that the extra computation is not worthwhile.

Whilst it is possible to describe light using words such as: 'wavelength', 'electromagnetic radiation', and 'coefficients of reflection', these must be interpreted as words of convenience, as they assist our understanding and attempts at describing the external world. Some experiments show that light travels in straight lines, whilst others confirm that it is bent by massive objects. Similarly, light can appear to spread as an undulating waveform, and on other occasions appear corpuscular in nature. These properties cannot concern us in computer graphics, therefore light is assumed to consist of simple rays of energy which undergo mechanical changes in direction when disturbed by a reflecting surface.

Figure 11.1 illustrates how a ray of light is diverted when it is reflected by a flat surface. Experiments confirm that the angle between the reflected ray and the surface normal (a line at right angles to the surface) is the same as that between the incident ray and the surface normal. This elementary observation can now be applied to the shading of computer images.

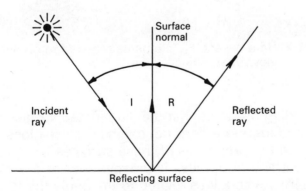

Figure 11.1 The angle of reflection equals the angle of incidence.

11.2 Flat shading

Flat shading is the simplest method of rendering a computer-generated image, but even this technique has two variations. If, for example, it was required to create a flat shaded view of a box, the following information is needed:

- the coordinate data describing the box;
- the position of the observer;
- the colour of the object;
- the position and colour of the light sources.

Figure 11.2 illustrates the geometry of the problem. Now if we can solve the problem of shading one side of the box, the entire box can be shaded by repeating the procedure for each side. So let us examine one isolated side as shown in Figure 11.3.

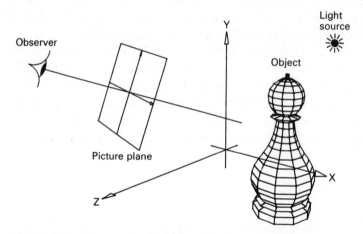

Figure 11.2 Here we see the elements required to obtain a shaded view of an object.

Flat shading assumes that the illuminated surface is a matt surface, and therefore does not exhibit surface gloss. Lambert investigated the properties of these surfaces, and discovered that the surface brightness is independent of the observer's position. However, it was related to the angle the light source made to the surface; in fact, it was directly proportional to the

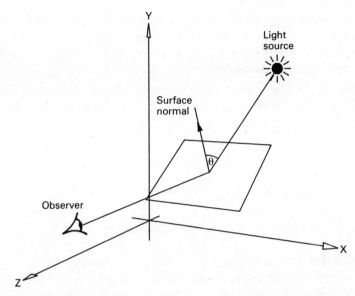

Figure 11.3 The brightness of a matt surface is proportional to the cosine of the angle θ, but independent of the observer's position.

cosine of the angle between the light source and the surface normal θ, as shown in Figure 11.3.

So here we have an excellent mechanism for shading. A computer program can easily undertake this calculation, and load numbers into a frame store representing the pixels covering this surface. If the frame store had three bytes for each pixel, i.e. red, green and blue, the actual numbers stored would be calculated as follows:

$$\text{red} = L_{red}.\text{Cosine}(\theta).C_{red}$$

$$\text{green} = L_{green}.\text{Cosine}(\theta).C_{green}$$

$$\text{blue} = L_{blue}.\text{Cosine}(\theta).C_{blue}$$

where L_{red}, L_{green} and L_{blue} are the amounts of red, green and blue in the light source, and C_{red}, C_{green} and C_{blue} are the coefficients of reflection for the surface.

But what happens if the light source shines directly across the surface making an incident angle of 90°? Theoretically the surface is not illuminated, and remains in shadow, which is how the above equations respond. But this would rarely happen in reality. There would always be a minimum level of ambient light, so the equations must incorporate the ambient light: A_{red}, A_{green}, and A_{blue}.

$$red = L_{red}.Cosine(\theta).C_{red} + A_{red}$$

$$green = L_{green}.Cosine(\theta).C_{green} + A_{green}$$

$$blue = L_{blue}.Cosine(\theta).C_{blue} + A_{blue}$$

But still the equations are very simple to compute.

Multiple light sources do not really upset the calculations, all that is required is for the program to accumulate the levels of red, green and blue from all the sources and load the frame store accordingly. Care must be taken to ensure the light levels do not exceed the system maximum, which is normally 255.

The second method of flat shading computes the colour changes that might occur across the surfaces of an object. The geometric calculations are very similar to those explained above, but this time the light levels are computed at each vertex, as shown in Figure 11.4. So that vertex A receives R_A, G_A, B_A; B receives R_B, G_B, B_B; and C receives R_C, G_C, B_C. Well, once these are known it is possible to compute any inter-mediate level along the eges AB, BC and CA, and ultimately any pixel upon the surface. Naturally this requires more computation, but the result is worth it. Plate 5 illustrates the effect of flat shading an object with two light sources.

11.3 Smooth shading

Smooth shading involves procedures for hiding the facets that comprise computer models. It is a mathematical operation, but I hope to explain it so that the reader can obtain some insight into the mechanism.

Frequently in computer graphics the concept of a surface normal is employed to explain certain geometric relationships.

This normal can be imagined as a stick pointing away from a surface at right angles,and can in fact be computed from the vertices comprising the surface.

If a box is drawn with these normals at every vertex, it would look like that shown in Figure 11.5. Within a program, each normal is stored by three numbers representing its X, Y, and Z-components. It is possible to compute an average normal at any vertex, which produces the situation shown in Figure 11.6.

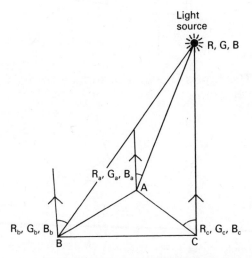

Figure 11.4 To improve flat shading, light levels computed at A, B and C are interpolated (averaged) along the edges AB, BC and CA. Pixel values for the facet can then be computed from these numbers.

Now if this object is shaded, and the average normals are used in the illumination calculations, when any side is shaded, the edges will have light values based upon the average normals rather than the surface normals. A consequence of this is that there will not be a sudden change of illumination as the shading program moves from surface to surface.

This type of shading is known as Gouraud shading after the inventor. Plate 6 illustrates a flat shaded and smooth shaded torus. Very little extra effort is required to incorporate these calculations.

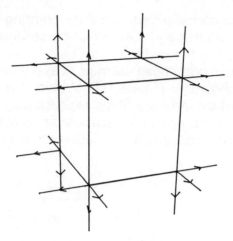

Figure 11.5 This box is shown with surface normals drawn at each vertex.

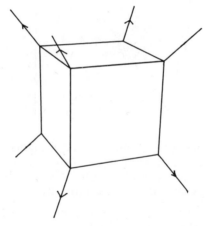

Figure 11.6 A view of a box with average normal vectors drawn at each vertex.

11.4 Phong shading

Flat shading—as the name suggests—creates a dusty matt surface, whilst smooth shading begins to introduce the hint of an eggshell sheen. In 1973 Bui Tuong Phong published his paper on 'Illumination for Computer Generated Images', in which he described the geometry and computation needed to create glossy surfaces. These programs have to undertake more calculations but the extra realism seems to be worthwhile.

To understand Phong shading, one must appreciate the mechanism behind the specular highlights observed in glossy surfaces. In Figure 11.7 I have shown a reflective surface illuminated by a light source. The observer will only see a reflection of the light source at the point P when the incident angle *In* equals the reflection angle *Rf*. If the observer moves, the specular reflection also moves.

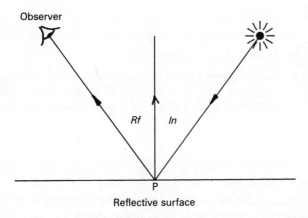

Figure 11.7 The observer will only see a specular highlight at P if the angle *In* equals *Rf*.

This geometry suffices for perfect reflectors, but what about real surfaces that spread the reflection over a finite area? This can be resolved by examining the situation illustrated in Figure 11.8. Here one sees the observer and light source just out of alignment for optimum reflection. The line M, is midway between the light source and the observer, and the angle α is used to control the specular light detected by the observer. Phong suggested that if a cosine was taken of α, the specular highlight would gradually disappear as the observer became increasingly misaligned. In fact, to force the highlight to disappear rapidly, he introduced a gloss parameter *n*, such that:

$$\text{specular light} \propto \text{cosine}^n \, \alpha.$$

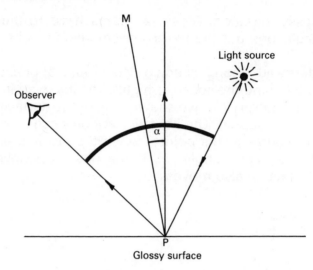

Figure 11.8 To compute the specular highlights it is necessary to calculate in 3D, the angle α, where the line PM is midway between the light source and the observer.

To achieve Phong shading, it is necessary to compute the surface normal at each pixel on the surface to discover α. This is substituted in the above and previous equations to ascertain the levels of red, green and blue light. Plate 7 illustrates a view of an object with four light sources using Phong shading.

It is worth observing the effect the gloss factor has upon the final image, so in Plate 8 I have illustrated three views of an object with different levels of *n*.

11.5 Shadows

The act of seeing and visual understanding is undoubtedly a complex process. In fact, a large proportion of the human brain is devoted to these tasks, and it has taken millions of years of evolutionary development to reach our sophisticated level of image processing. But apart from colour and shape, our comprehension of the real world is assisted greatly by the information contained in shadows.

Shadows—as everyone knows—are caused by illuminated surfaces being masked by other objects, and are a natural part of our everyday world. However, within the numerical world of the computer they do not occur naturally, they must be computed. Therefore, to enhance the realism of computer-generated images shadows can be incorporated, but they are an added cost in terms of programming effort and processor time.

The question now is how realistic should the shadows be? Because if one is searching for absolutely realistic images, the cost on all fronts is currently very high, especially for long sequences of animated images. If, on the other hand, a compromise is acceptable there are a number of acceptable solutions; here is one.

Figure 11.9 illustrates the geometric relationship between a light source, facet, surface and shadow, which points to the way a computer could be used to create shadows. Notice that the rays of light touching the corners of the facet construct a volume beyond its location, and if any other facet is within, or intersected by this volume, it will be in shadow. Obviously this

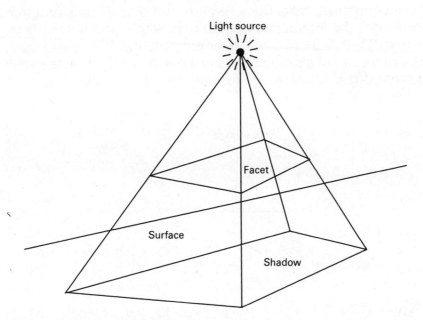

Figure 11.9 The geometric relationship between a light source, facet, surface and shadow.

can be undertaken by a program, but the calculations are lengthy.

A shadow edge is rarely a crisp straight line, because the source of illumination is never a singular point source. For even when a light source is a single lamp, there are normally · many other surfaces which introduce random reflections to create multiple shadows and a soft edge.

Recent research has suggested how soft edge shadows can be computed using shadow volumes with a Z-buffer (for hidden surface removal) but perhaps further work with ray tracing might prove the more rewarding.

11.6 Reflections

Another way of enhancing realism is to include reflected detail appearing in shiny surfaces, but again—as for shadows—this requires considerable extra computation. The technique of ray tracing accomplishes reflections, and resolves many other problems, but currently picture generation times are very long (one to several hours) on conventional computers.

Nevertheless, reflections require that a computer program simulates the interaction of light rays with a polished surface. Figure 11.10 illustrates the geometry involved in determining the reflection of a single object in a mirror. Notice that the view seen by the observer is formed by placing the object an

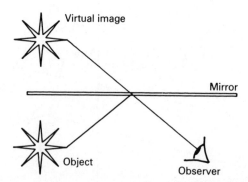

Figure 11.10 The virtual image seen by the observer, can be computed geometrically by placing the object an equivalent distance behind the mirror.

equivalent distance behind the mirror, and therefore involves very simple geometric calculations.

But the geometry is only part of the problem. What about accounting for the light absorbed by a reflective surface? How do shadows behave when cast upon a mirror? And how can multiple reflections be computed when several reflective objects are close to one another? These questions have been resolved but, as one might imagine, very clever programs are required.

11.7 Texture mapping

Texture mapping is a technique for covering computer models with surface detail. Early research workers would use the computer to create surrealistic pictures of teapots covered in a strawberry surface. This is achieved by storing inside the computer a coloured image of a texture, either from a photograph or paint system. The image is stored in pixel form which is scanned (manipulated geometrically), before being mapped into the frame store. Figure 11.11 illustrates this action.

One consequence of this mapping is that one pixel in the frame store may have several picture elements mapped into it,

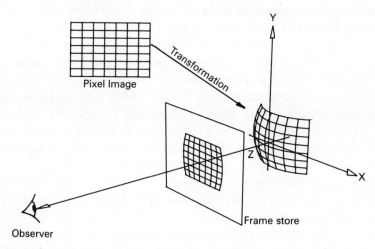

Figure 11.11 Texture mapping is achieved by scanning a pixel image and transforming its position geometrically, before loading it into a frame buffer.

which would cause aliasing. To overcome this, the relevant picture elements are processed such that the receiving pixel stores an average of the elements.

The Bosch FGS-4000 real-time animation system is capable of texture mapping video images upon its internal geometric models.

11.8 Hidden-surface removal

In Chapter 8, Section 6, I examined the process of hidden-line removal, which is concerned wtih the removal of edges that are totally or partially obscured by facets. In this section I will examine some of the ideas behind hidden-surface removal, which addresses the problem of shaded surfaces obscuring others.

Now if a computer is used to display a coloured image in a frame store, the program must ensure that shaded surfaces mask one another in a logical and natural way. There are a number of ways of achieving this, but I shall examine only three techniques.

Painter's algorithm

The painter's algorithm—as the name implies—employs a procedure employed by artists; that is, the image is formed by loading distant objects into the frame store, and loading others in turn as they become closer to the observer. Figure 11.12 shows this idea where the objects are shaded in the order C, B and then A. Unfortunately, the algorithm is not fool-proof, as sometimes inconsistencies arise in facet orientations. Consider the situation in Figure 11.13 where two facets, A and B, are orientated such that A is in front of B, and B is also in front of A. Obviously, the painter's algorithm would be unable to resolve this condition, therefore facets would have to be reduced to simple facets—perhaps triangles—before shading.

Notice how I have assumed that it is possible to sort facets into observer distance sequence. What is meant by the question, 'Is one facet behind or in front of another?' Really the test has only to be applied to facets which mask one another, which means that the painter's algorithm must include logic to resolve this masking condition. Figure 11.14 illustrates that only

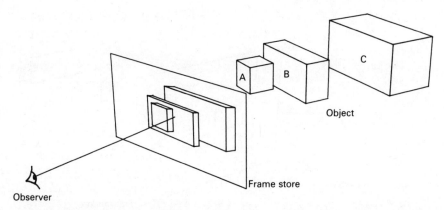

Figure 11.12 The painter's algorithm achieves hidden-surface removal by loading the furthest facets first, and the nearest last.

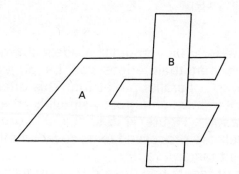

Figure 11.13 Facets A and B would prevent the painter's algorithm from shading them correctly, unless facet A was divided into two simpler facets.

facets B and C have to be sorted, as facet A is free of interference.

Scan-line algorithm

A television picture is created by displaying upon a phosphor screen a scanning spot which moves left to right, and top to bottom, in two sweeps in 1/25th of a second (United Kingdom) or 1/30th (United States). The scan-line algorithm employs a similar mechanism for computing a shaded picture.

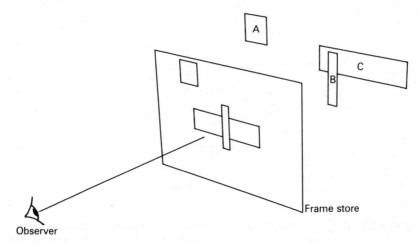

Figure 11.14 The painter's algorithm has only to sort facets B and C as they mask one another. Facet A can be shaded at any stage.

Basically, the internal computer models are rearranged and distorted such that their edges can be projected into the frame-store with a parallel projection. This effectively places the observer at infinity, and greatly simplifies the ensuing geometric calculations. Figure 11.15 shows this organisation and how the models are processed to discover whether they intersect the current raster line.

When a list of facets has been discovered which are cut by the raster line, they are sorted in depth sequence and shaded accordingly. Some specialist systems are able to perform this computation at the operating speed of television and consequently produce real-time pictures.

Z-buffer

The Z-buffer approach is cunningly simple, but does require large amounts of computer memory to operate. It works as follows: a piece of memory (Z-buffer) is initialised to store a very large numeric value for each pixel within the frame store. Facets are then shaded in any random sequence, but before the frame store is updated, the Z-buffer is examined to see if the new pixels are nearer than the previous ones; for the Z-buffer is used to hold the distance of the associated point to

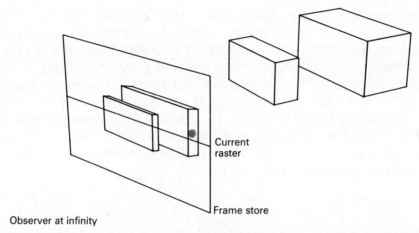

Current
raster

Frame store

Observer at infinity

Figure 11.15 The scan-line algorithm analyses the model space a line at a time, to determine the spatial relationship between facets, and their colours.

the observer in the Z-direction. If the point is nearer, the Z-buffer is updated and the frame store's values change, if not, the pixels are ignored.

Unfortunately, the Z-buffer cannot be used for transparent objects, as the facets are loaded in random order, and transparency calculations must have the opportunity of examining the physical relationships between objects.

Another method of achieving hidden-surface removal is by ray-tracing, but this will be examined in detail in Chapter 11, Section 10.

11.9 Aliasing and anti-aliasing

One major deficiency of low-resolution pixel-based systems, is that they exhibit aliasing errors when near horizontal or vertical edges are displayed. Figure 11.16 clarifies the problem by showing an enlarged portion of an edge stored within a frame store. This is often referred to as 'jaggies' or 'staircase effects'.

The aliasing is removed by anti-aliasing procedures which might be implemented within software or hardware. Either way it involves examining the pixels in clusters and arriving at an average central pixel value. This is called filtering and results in a softened image. Hardware systems such as the Bosch FGS-4000 and Quantel's Paint Box incorporate anti-aliasing in hardware. Another way to prevent aliasing, is to initially analyse the models to a higher resolution when shading, and then load an averaged value of the pixel into the frame store. Some film recorders draw at 8,000 lines per image and therefore aliasing is hardly detectable. Some colour display systems incorporate anti-aliased vectors to maintain a softer and more visually acceptable image.

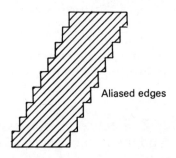

Aliased edges

Figure 11.16 Frame stores give rise to serrated edges ('jaggies' or staircase effects); this is called aliasing.

11.10　Ray tracing

Ray tracing or ray casting is a elegant method of shading computer images and copes with: shadows, reflections, hidden-surface removal, transparency and refraction. Amazing, one might think, but there is a slight problem, and that is that ray traced images have been known to take several hours to generate on conventional computers, which is why super computers such as the Cray X-MP are employed. Nevertheless, the technique is worth describing as recent research is identifying new ways of speeding up the calculations, and perhaps with the development of special hardware, ray tracing could be an important future technique in computer graphics.

The algorithm works as follows. If one imagines an observer looking through a frame store at a collection of objects as shown in Figure 11.17, one observes that only one ray can pass

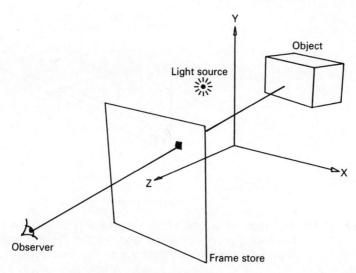

Figure 11.17 The basic idea behind ray tracing is that only one composite ray passes through any pixel to reach the observer's eye.

through a pixel and reach the eye. Therefore if it were possible to discover the ray's origins it would be possible to set the frame store's pixel levels.

But before considering the nature of colour levels, let us examine the problem of hidden-surface removal. To achieve this, for any given pixel a ray is traced back into the models being displayed. Where the ray intersects a facet, the distance to the observer is noted and the smallest distance identifies the nearest facet. Repeating this algorithm for each pixel produces a hidden-surface image when incorporated with light levels. Figure 11.18 illustrates this reasoning.

To compute the level of illumination at this nearest point, one would normally consider three components: the diffuse component, the specular component and any transmitted light for transparent objects. Unfortunately, there can be an infinite number of rays from difuse reflections and therefore they are not included in the calculations. Thus only specular and trans-mitted rays are considered.

For the specular component, the ray tracing program computes how the initial ray hit the surface, tracing it back in

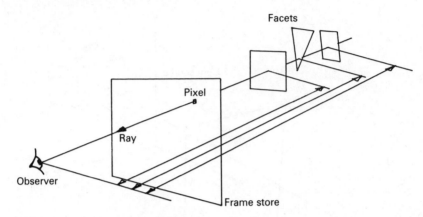

Figure 11.18 Ray tracing solves hidden-surface removal by tracing the intersection of a ray with all the facets, and then finding the smallest distance to the observer.

geometric history to find its origins. If it finally reaches a light source, it is possible to calculate the pixel's level of red, green and blue incorporating the losses incurred during its journey. If, on the other hand, the ray wanders away from the objects, an attenuated ambient background level can be assigned.

The transmitted component can incorporate colour absorption and refraction, providing realistic views of solid glass models.

The programmer must take care that the algorithm detects oscillating reflections, i.e. a ray that bounces back and forth between two facets, and fixes a limit to the depth of reflections examined. To achieve a complete image, the algorithm is applied to each pixel in turn, which is why it is so time consuming, as there can easily be 400,000 pixels to consider, or more.

The final image can also be anti-aliased by passing rays through the corners of each pixel to achieve an average colour level. But if these four boundary rays enclose a volume of space containing fine object detail, they too can be subdivided to improve the anti-aliasing.

Ray tracing methods have already been used in creating stunning animated images, and there may now be sufficient momentum in research programmes to produce dedicated systems incorporating this technique in hardware.

11.11 Summary

Considerable research effort has been devoted to the display of realistic shaded images, resulting in a number of excellent techniques, some of which are now appearing in firmware. Although designers will not personally become involved in using these methods, it is worth understanding the available techniques to appreciate their strengths and weaknesses. Here then is a summary:

- Light is assumed to travel in straight lines and obey the simple laws of reflection and refraction.

- It is not always necessary to take into account the attenuation of energy as light travels.

- Shading algorithms frequently employ the technique of colour separation into red, green and blue to compute the final colour of a surface.

- A program requires a colour to be given to an object and the sources of illumination.

- Flat shading employs Lambert's cosine law to shade an object's facets.

- The idea of ambient light is introduced to prevent surfaces that are not directly illuminated, to receive some level of background light.

- Smooth shading disguises the separate polygons by averaging the normal vectors at each vertex and is often called Gouraud shading.

- Phong shading incorporates specular highlights giving surfaces a glossy shine.

- Shadows can be computed by determining shadow volumes created by objects masking light sources.

- Reflections can be computed in reflective sufaces, and are a natural product of ray tracing.

- Texture mapping is concerned with mapping real or synthetic patterns over computer-generated images.

- Hidden-surface removal techniques include: the painter's algorithm, scan-line algorithm and the Z-buffer.

- Aliasing (jaggies or staircase effects) occurs when near vertical or near horizontal edges are stored within pixel-based systems, such as frame stores, but can be removed by anti-aliasing procedures to soften the edge.

- Ray tracing or ray casting, establishes the geometric history of any ray reaching the observer via a pixel, and solves the problems of: hidden-surface removal, shadows, reflections, refraction and specular highlights.

12 Colour peripherals

'The purest and most thoughtful minds are those which love colour the most.'

John Ruskin

The last decade has seen the development of a wide variety of equipment capable of capturing computer-generated images; and today it is possible to obtain colour pictures upon paper, plastic and film. But the growth of video has, in some applications, made conventional image-capture redundant. For if an image is to be ultimately broadcast as television, there is no need to store it on paper. It can be held digitally and converted into video format when needed.

However, graphics-based industries require a wide variety of media to store pictures and in this section paper, film and video are examined.

12.1 Colour plotters

As yet, there is no direct method of displaying coloured pictures upon paper, to the resolution of conventional photographs with thousands of colours. Nevertheless, not many applications require such a specification, which has resulted in a range of devices from colour hard copy units to large electrostatic plotters.

A hard copy unit such as the Tektronix 4692, can be connected to a variety of display terminals for printing the screen's contents upon an A4 sheet of paper. The image is constructed from a matrix of coloured dots to a resolution of 1,536 × 1,152. The copier employs ink jet technology, which sprays the image upon clay-coated plain paper or transparency film from cartridges of yellow, cyan, magenta and black. Applications for this type of device range from computer aided design to business presentation graphics.

Another method of producing coloured output upon paper relies upon a conventional graph plotter equipped with several coloured pens. Although this creates superb line quality drawings, the infill of areas of colour can only be achieved by single-hatching and cross-hatching of lines.

At the other end of the spectrum one finds Versatec's electrostatic plotter, which creates large E-size (34" × 44") sheets of coloured images constructed from a matrix of dots, 40,000 points per square inch. The image is formed by overprinting the primary printing colours using an electrostatic spray technique. Typically an E-size image takes eight minutes to create.

12.2 Colour film recorders

One very simple method of capturing a screen's image upon film, is to photograph it. This can be achieved with the aid of a rigid hood to minimize reflections and extraneous light. It works quite well and has even been used for serious animation purposes.

The major disadvantages of this approach is that generally the monitor's screen is curved and the raster is visible. To overcome these faults, firms such as Dunn Instruments and Matrix Instruments have developed devices which project the image upon a flat CRT screen, which is then photographed. To disguise the raster, the image can be 'shaken' electronically by approximately half the width of the raster; this is called dithering.

Furthermore, to improve the stability of the coloured image the picture is displayed in monochrome and photographed through colour filters of red, green and blue. Thus the true colour separations held in a frame store, can be displayed separately through the filters to form a composite coloured picture in 35mm, 16mm cine or Polaroid format. A photograph of the Dunn System is shown in Figure 12.1.

To achieve high-resolution pictures, it is necessary to use film recorders employing a scanning spot. The cathode ray tube (CRT) in these devices is very accurate, having a flat face glass, clean and free of bubbles, striations and other defects. As the resolution increases so the spot size must reduce, which creates various problems in the tube's design and

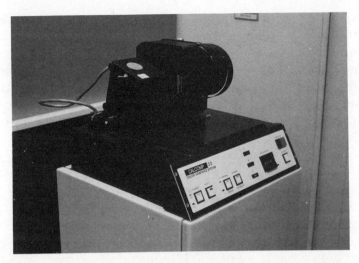

Figure 12.1 This Dunn camera can reproduce computer-generated images in 35mm slide, 16mm and 35mm cine and Polaroid formats.

manufacture. Typically, a spot size is about 0.001" and enables pictures to be displayed at 1,500 to 8,000 lines.

12.3 Video equipment

Many colour display devices have an output for video systems, which permits the recording of the images upon video tape. Naturally, this has had a tremendous impact upon computer animation, as it permits the direct output from a computer's frame store on to video tape.

One requirement, however, in using this approach to animation, is that the video recorder must be capable of registering a single frame. This is because a computer will generally require several minutes to load an image into the frame store. Using a special controller, conventional professional recorders can record single frames, with the aid of time code signals stored on the video tape. The disadvantage of this method is that the tape is continuously shuttling to and fro, placing the machine under considerable mechanical stress. This now has all changed, for recently, both Bosch and Sony have introduced single-frame 1" video recorders that record without shuttling the tape.

One device that is free of the mechanical weaknesses of tape recording is the magnetic video disk. This is capable of storing approximately 250 separate colour frames (10 seconds), and playing them back in real-time (25 fps in Britain and 30 fps in the United States).

The optical video disk scanned by a laser, is already part of everyday technology, but home use is restricted to read-only systems. The computer industry is just starting to use non-erasable optical disks for storage purposes. These have capacities in excess of 1 giga bytes (1,000 mega bytes) on a 12" disk. A smaller 5¼" disk is also available for personal computers with a capacity of 500 Mbytes.

In the next few years we are going to see the arrival of the erasable optical disk, which will transform the way we store information, whether it be text or graphics, and certainly it will have an impact upon computer graphics.

12.4 Summary

Frequently, computer graphic systems are employed to provide a temporary image to aid some design process. But ultimately, there comes a time when the image must be captured upon some useful medium. Graph plotters are ideal in displaying line artwork upon paper but coloured images require different technology. Here, then is a summary of the points raised in this section:

- Ink jet plotters are capable of printing images upon paper from A4 to A5, with a wide variety of resolution and colour combinations.

- Versatec's electrostatic plotters can produce E-size colour plots upon paper.

- Colour film recorders can capture coloured pictures on 35mm slide or cine, 16mm cine or Polaroid formats at resolutions from 512 to 8,000 lines.

- Video systems can record colour pictures upon video tape or video disk, continuously or as single frames.

- Optical disk systems are already available capable of displaying pictures at video rates, but in the future we expect the arrival of the erasable disk.

13 3D colour applications

'I believe in Michael Angelo, Velasquez, and Rembrandt;
in the might of design, the mystery of color, the redemp-
tion of all things by Beauty everlasting, and the message
of Art that has made these hands blessed.'

George Bernard Shaw

Ten chapters earlier, I was explaining the principles of
Cartesian coordinates as a mechanism for supporting computer graphics. Since those initial ideas we have discovered
how coordinates can be processed; how 3D models are constructed and manipulated, and how the physics of illumination
can be simulated to produce realistic three-dimensional
pictures. And today, 3D colour computer graphic systems are
finding their way into a number of diverse areas including
molecular modelling, business graphics, architecture, interior
design, shoe design, CAD and animation. And it is this last
area that I would like to expand upon, as it encompasses
virtually every aspect of 3D graphics to resolve its problems.

13.1 Animation

By now the reader should be under no illusions as to how
computers produce coloured 3D images. Every feature of the
final image must have been anticipated in the original programs, from the shape of the models, the colour and positions
of light sources, to the highlights, shadows and reflections.
Initially, this might seem a daunting task, but programmers
employ a variety of design aids to assist them in the construction of large programs.

One powerful technique employed in program design is
modularity; that is, never create a massive monolithic maze of
logic, but divide logical procedures into discrete modules.
These modules can then be tested individually, and once
debugged can be confidently used alongside previously tested
programs.

So what would be the building blocks for an animation system? Well, although the following list might not be totally complete, it does identify the major features.

Data base

A data base describes the organisation of data within a computer system. So in the context of animation it would determine how 3D models are stored. This might be in the form of a number of ways including faceted, procedural definition (described by rules), voxel definition (use of volume elements), or by solid modelling constructs. But the most conventional technique is using planar facets.

The data base must not only store the raw coordinates of the models, but the associated normal and average normal vectors required by the shading programs. It must also hold colour and surface properties such as: reflection coefficients, gloss factors, transparency coefficients and refractive indicies.

Apart from the models, the data base will also maintain the positions of light sources and their colour intensities, and whether they are flood, spot, ambient, etc.

Modelling procedures

A variety of modelling techniques must be available to permit the creation of the 3D elements to be animated. This might be in the form of internally held primitives, external coordinate definitions or with interactive construction by the user.

Scripting

As everything is held within the computer numerically, it means that these numbers can be changed dynamically. Therefore, basically anything may be changed within a computer program whilst it is running.

To control these changes, a script must exist within the system which identifies the values of parameters at specific key frames. Just imagine the things that could be changed and their impact upon the final animation:

- the size and position of every object;
- angular rotations of the objects;
- objects transforming into other objects;

- the focal point of the observer;
- the distance, rotation and elevation of the observer;
- the distance of the picture plane;
- the curvature of the picture plane;
- the positions of the light sources;
- the hue, saturation and value of the lights;
- the reflection coefficients of the object;
- the level of ambient light;
- the gloss, transparency and refractive index;
- texture mapping changes, etc.

All of these could alter simultaneously, but someone has to specify when and how. This would normally be in the form of a script of actions, and would be interpreted by the program which would also incorporate the cushioning and holds, to ensure that any alteration is smooth and realistic.

Line testing

Once the data base contains the relevant models and a script has been prepared, initial line testing is undertaken using simple wire frame models to verify the dynamics of any movements. Then simple shading tests can be made to ensure the effectiveness of light sources and resulting highlights and any shadows.

User interface

The more sophisticated the system becomes, the more important it is that the user is able to alter parameters with the minimum of effort. This aspect of a computer system is known as the user interface, and has given rise to names such as 'user friendly'.

The ultimate success of any computer graphic systems depends greatly upon this interface, for no matter how clever the internal programs are, unless a creative human being can communicate his or her artistic ideas, it is all rather futile.

To illustrate how some of these ideas can be programmed, consider the following commands found in a PICASO program:

```
CALL IN3D(MODEL, 'DATA3D')
```

This program inputs from a disk file a coordinate model called 'DATA3D', and is referred to as MODEL within the program.

CALL SHIFT3(MODEL, 0.0, 2.0, 0.0)

This program effectively shifts the model zero units in the X-direction, 2 units in the Y-direction and zero in the Z.

CALL PEYE(0.0, 0.0, 0.0, 20.0, 0.0, 30.0)

This statement establishes the position of the observer, looking at the 3D origin (X = 0.0, Y = 0.0 and Z = 0.0), 20.0 units distance, no rotation and 30.0° elevation.

CALL OBJCOL(MODEL, 0.0, 50.0, 75.0)

This statement sets the colour of MODEL to a hue of 0.0 (red), 50.0 per cent saturated, and a value of 75 per cent.

CALL LIGHTS(LAMPS, DETAIL)

This statement establishes the colours and positions of light sources held in DETAIL.

CALL PHONG(MODEL, LAMPS)

And this statement produces a PHONG shaded view of MODEL using the illumination specified by LAMPS.

Now these commands can be set up within a program, and all that is needed is for someone to give values to the variables, and then leave the computer to output its images upon tape, disk or film.

The above description might appear a little simplistic, and perhaps gives the impression that sophisticated animation can be achieved in several hours. This is far from the truth, because no matter how perfect a program is thought to be, they are generally riddled with logical bugs and inconsistencies that manifest themselves when the pressure is on. For in spite of the computer hardware being very reliable, the software—since it is a formulation of so-called human logical analysis—is always suspect, always ready to collapse at the most inopportune moment. Consequently, considerable effort is still required to produce trivial lengths of animated images, but tremendous strides are being made; every new project increases one's understanding of the subject and permits us to use it more creatively the next time.

13.2 Summary

Although I have only dealt with animation in this chapter, I hope it has given the reader an appreciation of the potential of 3D computer graphics. Here, then, are the major features of 3D colour systems:

- A variety of techniques are available for the storage of 3D structures, from simple facets to parametric definitions.

- Whenever a number is used to represent an attribute, quality, movement, size, position, etc. within a computer, it can be altered by the program to vary between any specified limits.

- Any changes taking place within a program can either be prepared in advance as a script in some suitable form, or altered interactively by a user whilst the program is working.

- Dynamic movements are often line tested whilst the images are in wire frame form.

- An important feature of any interactive computer graphic system is the user interface. The communication of ideas, in both directions, requires clever and sensitive programming.

14 Turnkey systems

'Variety's the spice of life,
That gives it all its flavour.'
William Cowper

As computer graphics has been adopted by a wide variety of disciplines, one has witnessed an increasing number of systems designed to address the specific needs of specialist design activities. In particular, there are turnkey systems for: graphic design, architecture, textile design, typesetting, 2D drafting, 3D modelling, shoe design, molecular modelling and animation.

This appears to be the natural way forward, as users of computer-based systems should not have to be distracted by the mechanism of bits and bytes that make it all possible. Ideally, the computer component of any system should be virtually transparent to the user, and the language of communication should be problem dependent. By this, I mean, systems should employ commands, messages, controls and menus that are understood directly by the user, without any need of extra translation. This imposes a tremendous responsibility upon the designers of these systems, because unless the underlying software includes these features, the system is doomed to a short life.

The fact that users of turnkey systems do not need to have programming skills, does not imply they need no training in their operation. Far from it. Some current systems are so sophisticated and powerful, that extensive training courses are necessary to enable users to exploit their potential. And in the author's own experience, unless a reasonably close contact is maintained with these devices, it becomes increasingly difficult to maintain a commanding hold upon their operation.

Some systems are conceptually very simple, but technically very complex. For example, paint systems basically require a frame store, processor, colour monitor, tablet and stylus and some very clever programs. Also, an architectural system only requires a general-purpose minicomputer, graphic screen, plotter, tablet and stylus, and once more some clever software. But there are instances where highly specialised equipment has been constructed to overcome the immense problems posed by the application area.

14.1 Real-time systems

In the area of animation, one of the principal aims is to make the computer create images within the refresh rate of the display system. This implies a rate of 25 fps (in Britain), or 30 fps (in the United States). This is possible in many monochrome applications, but demands powerful processors when coloured images are needed.

Just imagine the processing speeds required to fill a frame store (576 lines by 768 pixels) with three bytes (red, green and blue) for every pixel. And undertake lighting, shading and hidden-surface calculations, all within 1/25th of a second. Rather a tall order.

One way around this is to design a system dedicated to the task. Where graphic processes such as clipping, perspective, illumination and shading are undertaken by specific pieces of hardware. An example of this is the real-time animation system the FGS-4000 built by Bosch. This is capable of displaying perspective views of moving 3D models, Phong or flat shaded, illuminated, hidden-surfaces and texture mapped in real-time. But the real-time feature cannot hold for all models. For as they increase in complexity, so the refresh rate decreases. Nevertheless, it is an incredible feat for any piece of electronic equipment.

A similar specialist system is Quantel's MIRAGE, which can virtually apply any geometric transformation to a video image and produce stunning visual effects. But this machine is also programmable, and its library of effects can continuously be extended by the user, and ultimately only limited by his or her imagination.

The evolution of these systems has meant that designers can produce graphic effects literally in minutes, which might have taken days or weeks using conventional equipment. In some instances, general purpose computers could not have solved the problem.

Apart from turnkey systems, there is a new generation of display peripherals incorporating many of the graphic procedures described earlier within this book. Currently it is possible to purchase display systems incorporating sophisticated processors, called 'graphic engines', as they include within their microprocessors coordinate transformations, perspective, clipping, shading, modelling and hidden-surface functions.

This type of evolution will enable research and development into computer graphic applications to grow at an even faster rate, as they release the computer from many tedious software tasks, that are now sufficiently understood for them to be committed to hardware.

14.2 Summary

General-purpose computers do not always provide the best solution to the problems encountered in computer graphics. New silicon chips, dedicated to the tasks currently undertaken by software, are proving to be much more efficient.

The next generation of computer graphic equipment will operate at real-time speeds, and include most of the features discussed in previous chapters. Perhaps, eventually even a ray tracing processor might be developed.

So the points to remember are:

- General-purpose computers are used as the basis of many turnkey systems for specialist users.

- General-purpose computers find it very difficult to maintain real-time animated colour images.

- Specialist turnkey systems such as the Bosch FGS-4000 can achieve real-time shaded animation on certain models.

- Ultra high-speed digital video systems like Quantel's MIRAGE, can perform unbelievable geometric tricks with any video source in real-time.

- New terminals and workstations are currently available which incorporate many of the graphic procedures currently achieved by software.

15 Conclusions

'Wisdom is rooted in watching with affection the way people grow.'

Confucius

One objective of this book was to survey the area of two-dimensional and three-dimensional computer graphics, and explain the subject from a non-technical standpoint. Another was to bring home to the designer how the computer has to be programmed to create the slightest graphical effect. I may have been successful in both objectives. But where does this leave the designer? I believe it leaves the designer where he or she always was, responsible for inventive and creative design ideas, but with a rather special assistant.

The computer, as we have seen, is an amazing machine, perhaps the most revolutionary concept the human intellect has produced. But certainly not the last. Remember, just forty years has lapsed since ENIAC was built, and it was only 1962 when Sutherland presented his paper on 'Sketchpad'. Yet today, computer graphics has been elevated to such a position, that one has the impression there is no longer any need for design, the work is all undertaken by computers. Any designer who has read and understood the previous chapters will have appreciated that these systems are unable to design. They are blind machines constructed with an uncanny perfection, but driven by software incorporating every aspect of human logical frailty.

Perhaps this is rather harsh, but it is true. Needless to say, I still believe that computer graphics is one of the most exciting, creative, stimulating and important developments of twentieth-century technology. But let us keep its role within design in perspective.

Those designers who have already started to use computers have perhaps sensed the latent potential within computer graphics, and probably found it difficult to bring to the surface. I do not believe this to be the fault of the designer. This is a characteristic of the computer graphic profession. For it still has not had sufficient time to stand alongside other disciplines with a reliability and confidence like subjects such as photography. Its immaturity is still evident and if too much is expected from this technological juvenile, we will all be very disappointed.

Personally, I see computer graphics as a child raised all of its life within the secure environment of research laboratories, lovingly cared for by parental programmers. And today, it is taking its first nervous steps into the commercial jungle of design, where it will be watched carefully by equally nervous designers.

Occasionally, it will be used to create banal graphics, and will get the blame. Equally, it will produce stunning, exciting images and be denied recognition. But I believe eventually it will find its natural place alongside other systems and enjoy a healthy life, and eventually we will all wonder what the fuss was about.

Further reading

If the reader wishes to enhance his or her knowledge on the artistic or technical aspects of computer graphics, the following books are recommended:

Foley, J. D. and Van Dam, A.,
Fundamentals of Interactive Computer Graphics,
Addison-Wesley, 1982.

Harrington, S.,
Computer Graphics: A Programming Approach.
McGraw-Hill, 1983.

Hunt, R. W. G.,
The Reproduction of Colour,
Fountain Press, 1975.

Jankel, A. and Morton, R.,
Creative Computer Graphics,
Cambridge University Press, 1984.

Newman, W. M. and Sproull, R. F.,
Principles of Interative Computer Graphics,
McGraw-Hill, 1981.

Pavlidis, T.,
Algorithms for Graphics and Image Processing,
Springer-Verlag, 1982.

Prueitt, M. L.,
Art and the Computer,
McGraw-Hill, 1984.

Scott, J., ed.,
Computergraphia,
Gulf Publishing Co., 1984.

Vince, J. A.,
Dictionary of Computer Graphics,
Frances Pinter, 1984.

Wexley, G.,
Colour Vision (Units 10–11),
The Open University Press, 1981.

Index